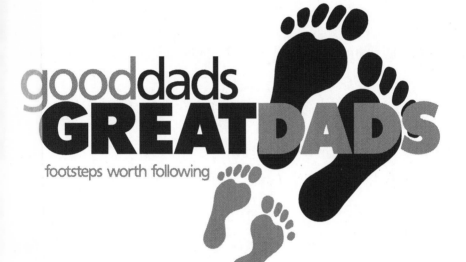

good dads
GREAT DADS
footsteps worth following

Copyright, Good Dads GREAT DADS. 2013

Good dads Great Dads
10 Clare st Croydon South, Victoria, 3136, Australia

National Library of Australia Cataloguing-in-Publication entry

Author: White, Mal, author.

Title: Good dads great dads : footsteps worth following / Mal White.

ISBN: 9780992278007 (paperback)

Subjects: Fatherhood.

Fathers.

Parenting.

Father and child.

Dewey Number: 306.8742

I dedicate this book to my three sons; Jordan, Jesse and Josiah.
You have taught me how wonderful it is to be a dad.

In memory

William Harold James White
Born in Cwmgwrach, Wales 29/ 9/1933
Died Skipton, Australia 26/11/1988

To my dad, I wish with all my heart you did not die so young.
We would have been good friends.
Thanks for believing in me, loving me and taking me fishing.
My heart still yearns for you.

Mal

Acknowledgements

I would like to thank the following people;

My lovely wife Karen. You have taught me how to love and be loved.

Bev, my dear mother for your love and support.

My brother Steve for your friendship and love.

Tim Costello for encouraging me many times and writing the great foreword for this book.

Marylin Leermakers. Building KIDS HOPE with you was a major highlight in my life.

I am forever indebted to the following people for supporting me during my battle with Leukemia;

Chris Danes, Phil Bosua, Nick Krins, Geoff Groube, Rick Batchelor, Wayne Nebauer, Bob and Calvin Salomons.

Contents

Foreword by Tim Costello

I thank Mal White for the gift he is offering with this incredibly thoughtful yet practical work. Mal has tapped into a deep well of reflection and wisdom. I know that many will find this book a valuable help in enhancing their journey towards becoming 'great dads'.

Australian literature is replete with stories of absent dads, from Henry Lawson's tales of courageous women battling to raise poor kids with a missing father, to the modern day phenomenon of workaholic absent fathers. Yet fathering is a man's most important calling. Seeing children grow and thrive is life's greatest reward, and the rising of new generations is what moves humanity forward. This is a book that addresses the task of being a father, and it is inspiring.

I find it encouraging that more and more fathers are taking a much more active role in parenting – something incredibly positive for the fathers, their partners and their children alike. But being a parent isn't always easy – knowing what to do doesn't always come naturally. All kinds of circumstances can make the job harder, especially for those parenting alone, or who are separated from their partners. So it really matters that fathers share their experiences and learn from each other. Hopefully this book will make a real difference to many men struggling to make the most of the unique privilege and opportunity that fatherhood gives us.

Growing up I was fortunate to be very close to my own father – who for a few years I saw every day at school as well as at home. He was a powerful yet humble role model – a teacher by vocation, and truly a teacher by nature. He conveyed to me so much about love and belonging, about responsibility and care, and also about the joy of life. He was always an encouraging voice, nurturing care and curiosity about the world, and affirming all of us as we faced life's big challenges and questions. He shared equally an enthusiasm for robust discussion about the issues of the day, and an unbridled love of sport.

Like many parents in today's world, my own experience of fatherhood has been very closely bound up with a demanding work life. Life has brought many fascinating travels and experiences, but of all the roles one can fill in life, I remain certain that nothing can come close in terms of satisfaction and reward than being with one's children as they grow to adulthood.

I thank Mal White for the gift he is offering with this incredibly thoughtful yet practical work. Mal has tapped into a deep well of reflection and wisdom. I know that many will find this book a valuable help in enhancing their journey towards becoming 'great dads'.

Introduction

All dads need encouragement. Most of us have room for improvement in our fathering skills. Many of us want the absolute best for our kids. The fact that you are reading this tells me that you are a good dad and like many good dads, we ask, "How do we become great dads?" Join our online community of good dads becoming great dads. http://www.facebook.com/gooddadsgreatdads Like us on Facebook for daily inspiration.

My wife and I sat with our three sons at the dinner table. I was not looking forward to telling them our sad news. It was April 30, 2007. Earlier that day I had been diagnosed with Leukemia.

Being diagnosed with bone marrow cancer came as a damaging blow to me at the age of 42. But where it hit me the hardest was in the dad zone. Telling my three young teenage sons that their dad has cancer was the most internally churning experience of my life.

I knew fatherhood was important to me, but in that moment, I realized that being a dad meant everything to me.

Fatherhood is the most awesome thrill and privilege a man can share with his partner. And, along with the joys, there are many challenges added to the mix.

Being a great dad is not an auto response once we bring the baby home from hospital. We don't have a default setting that allows us to be automatically awesome dads. We need vital input along the way. It is my hope that this book will inspire and encourage you in a very practical way to be the great dad you were destined to be. May it add to your effectiveness as a very involved dad, resulting in your children having the best opportunity to become everything they can be in this life.

Many men are instinctly good at being dads. Some are great dads. Some dads have made a total effort to be highly engaged and effective in their role as fathers. Others have been distracted or caught up in other activities.

In our fast paced and demanding world, how do we ensure that when we have children, we will be what they need us to be? How do we know if we will be effective in their development? How will we measure up as fathers? What things will we do differently from how our fathers raised us? What will we do the same? What will our relationship with our children be like when they grow up? What can we do about that now? When all is said and done, will we have been good dads or will we have been great dads?

Here are three different scenarios. The first two dramatically represent attitudes and lifestyles resulting from a lack of meaningful and involved fathering. In contrast, a significantly different situation was recently highlighted to me as my wife and I attended the funeral of a long-time family friend.

Michael, known as "Temmo", seemed like a reasonable person when you spoke with him one on one. But when he was with his gang he became a wild child. How could one 15 year old cause so much damage to public property and not get caught? He was a reliable source of dope and harder stuff if you needed it but "you had better keep your bloody @#$@#$ mouth shut if you know what's %@#$%$ good for you!"

Temmo ran with the pack. He felt bigger, stronger and more important when he was with the gang. He felt more masculine when they were smashing a bus stop to pieces or spraying graffiti along someone's newly constructed brick fence, or one of his favorites, setting fire to the local scout hall.

Why had Michael become so delinquent? Why did he feel the need to wreak such havoc and why did he have this insatiable need to feel bigger or more important? His mother had no control over him and she felt deeply wounded by his lack of respect for her.

His dad was a nice enough sort of bloke, he worked hard to provide for the family. He meant well. His own father had not related very closely or affectionately toward him, and he in turn didn't really know how to relate very well to his son, Michael. It was awkward trying to be anything other than a provider, so he just left the " personal stuff" up to "mum".

Why is it so difficult to be an effective dad when most of us want the very best for our kids?

Angel worked in an inner brothel. She was 19. It had never been her intention to end up here. Her first sexual encounter was at 12 and by fourteen she was sexually active. At 15 she was pregnant. She longed for masculine love. She longed for someone to love her and affirm her to make her feel like a princess. She felt empty inside, yearning for someone to fill the emptiness in her life. Her dad had been there, but had never really connected with any of his four children. He had never said the words she longed to hear, "I love you" or "you're my princess." Awkwardly, he quietly left for work each morning, came home, ate his evening meal and then went out to the shed where he pottered till bedtime. Though he was around, he was a completely disconnected and an absent father for Angel.

Dads have such a powerful influence in the lives of their children. Our family of origin has such a strong bearing on who we become in life. How will your children turn out? What will be their home-life experience and how will it shape who they become as adults? In their relationship to you their father, will they be thankful or will they be forever conscious of the gaps in your relationship, forever looking elsewhere to have their needs met?

Bill passed away at 83. The church service was a truly unique celebration of a life well lived. His five sons led the proceedings, which in itself was a rare occurrence. But to then have each one speak so sincerely about the rich, father-son relationship they had enjoyed with their dad and his investment in their lives, left me both inspired and envious.

What made Bill such an effective father in the lives of his five sons?

All dads need encouragement. Most of us have room for improvement in our fathering skills. Most of us want the absolute best for our kids. Most of us are good dads but how do we become great dads?

Good dads GREAT DADS is written to encourage you in one of the most important jobs on the planet, raising great kids. It is written especially for dads. If you are not a dad, you are still most warmly welcomed among my pages. I am confident you will find the read a rich experience as I share many real life stories that I'm sure you will relate to.

There are many parenting experts and many great child-psychologists, researchers and academics in our nation. We can learn so much from them. I hold these people in high regard as they promote active fatherhood and parenthood. Some of these have influenced my thinking a great deal in my quest to be a better father.

I am not an academic and certainly do not claim to be an expert. I simply consider myself a dad that learned a lot from these highly educated people and applied what I learned in raising three children. I am now delighted to pass on to you what I have experienced and learned what works and what does not. As you read Good Dads GREAT DADS, you will quickly discover that I am a practical person and quite open about my experiences firstly as a son and then as a father.

There are some things I got right in raising children and some aspects I could have done much better. I realize I cannot turn the clock back and re-do those areas. Most of this book is about how to be more effective in your relationship with your children and how to invest in your child's development. You only get one opportunity to raise each child. The more you get right, the less you will feel the need to rewind the clock seeking to repair damage done.

I was privileged to work for World Vision for a number of years helping to establish a national mentoring program for primary school children needing additional support. Through exposure to hundreds of schools and hearing so many stories about children I was confronted first hand with how important the role of parents are in the formative years of their children.

My involvement with the KIDS HOPE program taught me much about the social and emotional developmental needs of children and I have no doubt that it fuelled my passion for the promotion of effective parenthood. I make several references to my experiences as a KIDS HOPE staff member throughout the book.

I can do little for Temmo and Angel, but I can encourage other fathers to truly be there for their own children and to provide practical ideas that will improve their communication and their lifelong relationship with their children.

I believe we can learn a great deal from each other as dads. I know I learn so much from my audiences and workshop participants. Someday I may have the opportunity to learn from and be inspired by you. I look forward to that.

I am grateful to my three children for teaching me that being a dad really is one of the greatest joys a man can know in this life. I am thankful to my very supportive wife, Karen who has encouraged me over 27 years of marriage to be a great dad. I am indebted to friends that have provided editorial comment on the manuscript for this book and grateful to Tim Costello, a man I respect deeply, for writing the foreword and for both believing in me, and giving me some timely encouragement along the way.

Finally I am thankful to my dad for being my dad, to my big brother Steve who at times has offered fatherly love and to the men throughout my life that have been mentors, friends, brothers and father figures. Wayne, Chris, Phil, Ron, Colin, Calvin, Bob, Nick, David, Rick, Geoff, Dave; you have all added so much to help me be a better man and a better dad.

One of my grandfathers died of Leukemia, one died of a heart attack. Both were way too young to die. My step grandfather died of old age.

My own father had open-heart surgery at forty-two and died at fifty-five of a heart attack. He was too young to leave us. Four years ago, I was diagnosed with Leukemia and I still have ongoing treatment. Life can be too short for far too many people. I hope to live a long and healthy life as much as the next bloke. Making the most of what we do have is what is important.

When confronted with a potentially life threatening disease such as blood cancer you are clearly stopped in your tracks. The aspect of my life where the pain felt the greatest was in relation to my three sons. When you are a dad there is a deep desire for your children to have a great life. In my case I wanted it to include me in it. Telling my three sons at the dinner table on the night of my diagnosis was the hardest thing I have ever had to do.

I believe that this whole four-year experience for me has been the catalyst to want to reach out and encourage other dads to make the most of the time they have with their children. My journey as a dad continues and thankfully, my illness is under control with medication. However, for me there remains a sense of urgency to get a message out there. A message that motivates and encourages other men in their relationships with their children. Kids need great dads. Someone either gave you this book for your inspiration or you have purchased it in good faith that it will benefit you and your children.

This book is an action manual. Read the contents and then take action. Kids need all the love and support they can get to be emotionally strong, resilient and to reach their full potential in life. They require you to be the best dad you can possibly be.

Allow me to reiterate, it is my aim to inspire and encourage you in a very practical way to be the great dad you were destined to be for the sake of your wonderful children and the rest of their lives.

Enjoy.

From Good to Great

In the past many men have had to toughen up due to war, high mortality hardship and the brevity of life. They learned to hide or suppress their emotions in order to survive. This stifled their relatability to women and children. Generations of emotionally impoverished men fumbled their way through relationships and opted for the hunter-gatherer role within the household, leaving the emotional, relational and social development and maturing of the children up to the mothers and mostly female classroom teachers.

This emotional and relational lack is passed from one generation to the other until someone consciously decides to break the cycle.

One of my all-time favourite songs is Cats in the Cradle. I love it.

When Harry Chapin penned those immortal words with his wife, I wonder if he had any idea just how enduring his song would be. Many are familiar with Cat Stevens' very popular version.

On occasion I sing this song with my guitar and often enjoy listening to it on the radio and my ipod. I wonder what was behind the lyrics? What had fuelled such an inspirational and enduring piece? I sense the writers' personal longing for more of his own dad in his life. There is a strong tone of lament in this legendary song. There is a sense of regret that the years have passed and the longing for connection with dad remains. There is a possible sense of regret that his own dad was too busy to spend time with him. In one live performance, available online, Harry relates the song to his relationship with his own son.

The words of that song speak loudly into my own life.

My father died at 55 years of age. I was 24. Occasionally I visit the cemetery where his capstone remains. "Here lies William Harold James White. Beloved Husband to Beverley and Father to Stephen, Julie, Maldwyn and Sandra."

In case you are wondering, my full name is Maldwyn. I was named after my father's best friend back in Wales, who was killed in a motorcycle accident only weeks before I was born. I was named in his memory.

As I sit by my father's gravesite I shed a tear. I miss him. I remember the good times and I long for more of him in my life. My dad was a good father, but he, like so many of his generation was not much into communicating his feelings or showing much emotion or affection. I remember trying so hard to get his affirmation and recognition. I went to great lengths to win his approval. I remember building up my muscles, training very hard in martial arts, and then calling him into my room to show him my newly developed skills, always looking for him to be impressed with me and what I could do.

I needed him to notice me and to be proud of me. I am confident that he was proud of me and I am sure, if he had lived, he would have approved of how I turned out as a man and as a father with my own children.

However, as a boy growing up, I just needed him to express his pride in me and let me know that I measured up. The occasional hand on the shoulder, a hug or a hand shake supported with a couple of loving words would have meant so much to me. I'm sure they would have made a significant difference as I was growing up and I think they would have had a lasting affect in my development into manhood. I look back to when he was alive and I wish he had been far more involved in my life and more emotionally connected to me than he had been. I wish he could have expressed his feelings toward me and showed me his fatherly affection.

I don't blame him for the shortfall and there is nothing I could do to strengthen our relationship once he died. All I knew I had the power to do was attempt to be more involved and connected with my own children. And now having raised them, I seek to encourage other men to be highly effective in their children's lives and where possible, to reach out to their own fathers in an effort to build on their relationship.

I know that I have spent my adult life striving to win the approval of others and being driven to achieve so that I could somehow get the acknowledgement from others that I had longed for as a child. I now understand that many men have had similar experiences to my own.

Children need, and long for, connection with their dads. They have an inbuilt desire to please both mum and dad and they need to know that they matter deeply to you. When a dad sits down and reads a story, plays a board game, kicks the ball in the backyard or simply sits down and watches their child strum on the guitar or bash away on the drums, it communicates many positive messages to their child.

Some of the messages include:
• I love being with you,
• You are a great person to spend time with;
• I'm glad you're my daughter or son,
• Nothing else is more important to me than simply hanging out with you.

Other messages conveyed are:
• I admire your skill and determination,
• I'm proud of you,

- You're funny,

- You've got what it takes,

- You belong to me,

- You are a very important part of this family.

In the past many men have had to toughen up due to war, high mortality hardship and the brevity of life. They learned to hide or suppress their emotions in order to survive. This stifled their relatability to women and children. Generations of emotionally impoverished men fumbled their way through relationships and opted for the hunter-gatherer role within the household, leaving the emotional, relational and social development and maturing of the children up to the mothers and mostly female classroom teachers.

This emotional and relational lack is passed from one generation to the other until someone consciously decides to break the cycle. Being emotionally and relationally intelligent is about being more aware of ourselves and more relatable to the people around us. These are essential ingredients in effective relationship building.

Fortunately most of us in the West are not engaged in overseas combat or other conflict that removes us from our families. However there are other threats and societal pressures that threaten to erode the family and deprive men of their emotional and relational strength and connection. Addiction to work, a desire for material possessions and financial security or a need to prove something, drive many men and women into incredible imbalances in their lives.

Imbalanced lives can often mean children miss out on our very best. Many children are underfathered and under nourished emotionally and relationally due to dad simply not being around and involved enough. Many children are growing up in relational poverty. One school principal suggests that many have emotional cheque-books that are completely overdrawn. Sometimes material items are given to children of all ages to appease the parent's sense of guilt for not truly being there.

A friend of mine, who is a reformed alcoholic and now professional counsellor, told me that he observes a strong parallel between people that have an alcohol addiction and people that are workaholics. He explained how both alcoholism and workaholism negatively affect the relationships with those people closest to them. His observation, from working with hundreds of individual addicts and also many couples, is that "workaholism" is a far greater indictment on our society and a greater threat to the family than alcoholism.

What price do we pay by working so much? Our lives are consumed by work. Should work be that important? Weren't we meant to work to live, not live to work?

Many years ago I heard a speaker referring to our nation as "The Land of the Long Lost Father". I feel shame to think we have stooped that low as a culture. It is desperately wrong, and I have seen the dysfunction in thousands of children's lives as a result of having an absent father. Big work commitments have deprived many children the contact with their fathers they desperately need. Low self-esteem, underachievement at school, misbehaviour and poor social skills immediately spring to mind as some of the evidences of under-fathering or father absenteeism.

In my work as a Life Coach and Executive Coach, I am very familiar with the common theme of adults spending their life trying to fill the gap that should have been, and can only be filled by their affirming, emotionally connected and truly present father. For my money, the biggest losers, when dad is a workaholic, or he's too busy doing other things rather than being a dad, are children.

Even though Harry Chapin penned his song over forty years ago, it continues to make an impact time and time again. Just this week I sang the song as part of an address to an audience of school parents. The affect on people's faces was obvious as they listened to the words and music of this powerful song.

My own personal journey of being a child with a dad and then becoming a father of three children has given me a perspective on the importance of getting fatherhood right. Being a dad for over twenty years and working professionally with hundreds of children, teens and families has led me to write this book and establish an organisation to encourage dads to be all they can be for the sake of their children. It is an important message that we all need to be encouraged with.

The message that dads are vital in their children's lives, and that switched on, in tune, emotionally connected, great dads are in high demand. You absolutely matter in your children's lives and this is a message that all dads far and wide need to hear.

When we take stock and ask ourselves what is most important to us, most people say that it is their family. Visit any cemetery and read a dozen head stones. There are no records of work achievements, ladders climbed or assets accumulated. There is usually only a small list of names engraved. These are the names of the deceased's immediate family members. These are the people who will matter in the end. Make sure they matter now while you can do something for them.

Ask any cancer patient in hospital about their priorities. Ask any heart attack victim what changes they are going to make in their life going forward. It is amazing how priorities are reorganized when tragedy strikes. The encouragement in this book is to look at your priorities now, not waiting till tragedy strikes and being sure you are doing all you can to be the difference in your children's lives, while you have the opportunity.

It is my great hope that as you read this book, you will think deeply about your own priorities and consider how you may adjust your schedule and focus, where applicable, so that your children are given every ounce of your fullest and most excellent fathering. This is what they need for their healthy development and for their best shot at life. They, like you, will only have one upbringing and only one chance to live life to the full. How can you make sure, as their dad, it is the best it can possibly be?

Harry Chapin was not alone in his lament for more time with his dad. May it never be said of your children that they missed out on all they needed from their dad because he was just too busy.

Important note to mothers: Most mothers also contribute to these basic needs for survival, of course, and in many cases mums have to take up much of this responsibility as well as the bulk load of emotional, social and relational nurture of children. Please understand that this book is purely aimed at encouraging men to be more proactive that they may enjoy increased effectiveness in their children's lives and development.

Most mothers are amazing. Most of us dads need reminding or confronting about the importance of our role. I am solely focussed, in this book, on the influence of fatherhood in the lives of children. Perhaps you know someone that may be encouraged by this book. I hope you enjoy the read and, of course, there will be many applications in this book that relate directly to motherhood as well as fatherhood.

If you are separated as parents, there are many ways you can compliment each other's relationship with your children. It is not a competition to see who is the best parent or who can get the highest level of the children's affections. Their overall development as human beings is what is important.

If you both read this book you may find ways to increase your effectiveness as parents, both individually and in cooperation with each other. I fully respect the challenges involved and have walked this journey with a number of friends.

Be encouraged that whilst the load of childraising is full-on at times, it is potentially the greatest joy and privilege in life. Once the hard yards are behind you, there is a lifetime to enjoy a meaningful relationship with your kids and maybe one day, their kids as well.

Let's see what we can do to ensure dads and kids enjoy the same life-long meaningful relationship with each other as well.

Maslow's Hierarchy of Needs.

When we look at the work of world-renown Psychologist Maslow, we have a frame of reference to help us determine how much of our child's development we have been involved in and how much we need to be involved in. This is commonly called Maslow's hierarchy of needs.

To assist you with a visual presentation, simply tap here to view Maslow's hierarchy.

Maslow's hierarchy is presented as a pyramid beginning at the bottom rung with our physiological need. Physiologically to survive we need the basics; breathing, food, water, and shelter.

The second tier in the hierarchy of human need is Safety. Maslow determines that each human being needs security of body, security of employment and security of resources. He also states that we need a reliable structure of morality and we need the reliability of the family, of health and of property.

Most dads meet these basic needs for human survival. As hunters and gatherers we generally do ok in providing shelter, food and protection.

The third level is Love and belonging. The need for friendship, family, sexual intimacy.

The fourth is Esteem. Self esteem, confidence, achievement, respect for others and respect by others.

The fifth and final level in the hierarchy in ascendency is self-actualization. This triangle completing the pyramid contains such human need as morality, creativity, spontaneity, problem solving, a lack of prejudice and acceptance of facts.

It is my belief that a father that has invested much time and energy into their child's formative and developmental years will have gone a long way to helping shape their child's life.

When a dad has been involved in their child's life through constant and regular contact and meaningful engagement, their child stands a far greater chance to develop strength and maturity in the top three levels in Maslow's hierarchy.

For a person to develop emotional and relational intelligence, social competence and personal confidence, together with resilience for overcoming hardships and the ability to solve problems in life they require the valuable input from others. Children need the input of mothers and fathers. Where this is not possible, they need the regular and consistent input from significant others for their holistic development.

Switched on dads that know how to spend time with their children, who know what to say and when to say it and understand the incredible value they bestow on the development of their child's life are the single most influential people on the planet. I call these men GREAT DADS!

Perhaps the opposite is also true. I heard of one speaker at a conference declaring that every major problem in the world including war and other atrocities committed against human beings are a result of poor fathering or serious underfathering.

Good dads provide the basics in a child's life as seen in the bottom two levels in Maslow's Hierarchy of Human need. GREAT DADS invest on a much more personal and consistent level over many years so that their children achieve a far deeper sense of love and belonging, esteem and self-actualization in accordance with the hierarchy.

This book is dedicated to good dads worldwide. Good dads that would like to be great dads. Good dads that are keen to learn, grow and are committed to investing in their children's lives and their relationship with them.

This book consists of a range of highly practical things we can be doing with our children to boost their self-esteem and self worth. Whilst it is great to spend time with the whole family on outings, holidays and family fun nights, much of my focus is on the one to one aspect of parenthood. Whilst this may be a juggling act for you to find quality one to one time with each child, you will discover why we need to make this a huge priority in being highly effective dads.

Each chapter is dedicated to a specific relationship building activity that we can apply with each of our children. When you implement these parenting essentials you will be investing more intentionally in your child's healthy development as a human being and also making a wise deposit in your relationship bank with them. An account you may look forward to drawing on for the rest of your life.

How your children will view you and relate to you in 10-20 years from now will, in all probability, be a reflection of the time spent with your children and the conscientious effort you make as a dad whilst they are in your care.

This is an investment well worth making. Many men I have spoken with are proud to be dads. Many dads have been caught off-guard by how quickly the years have passed them by. They can't believe their children are now living independent adult lives. Don't let the years creep up on you or be stolen from you. Be proud to be a dad. Be proud to spend lots of time with your children. Be proud to tell your kids how you feel about them.

When the day of leaving the proverbial nest finally arrives, and you watch your child drive slowly out of your driveway, with all their belongings crammed into the back of their small car, be able to stand proud with a tear in the corner of your eye, knowing that you were the best dad you could possibly have been for your children.

"When ya' comin' home dad? " "I don't know when, but we'll get together then son, you know we'll have a good time then."

CHAPTER 1

Do Something

Scheduling time to do something with your child is such a high value priority. Whilst regular interaction on a daily basis is important for nurturing the bond between you and your child, specially planned, one to one activities add a unique dimension to your relationship.

On one of our regular father and son dates we chose to go indoor rock climbing.

I remember enjoying a great trust-building time with my youngest son while he scaled the mammoth vertical wall with me as I provided the essential anchor down below.

It was a great opportunity to encourage him in his athleticism, confidence and climbing ability. His smile trumpeted his joy when he finally reached the roof, some 20 metres off the ground. It was after many attempts to build his confidence and climbing skill.

I still recall to this day his delight and sense of accomplishment in that precious moment, even after eight years have passed. It was a significant father and son outing for sure.

The attendant asked us if my son had the day off school. I replied simply, that each of my sons gets to have one day off per term to have a father and son day with me.

She immediately responded with a tone of lament, "I wish my dad had done that with me!"

Scheduling time to do something with your child is such a high value priority. Whilst regular interaction on a daily basis is important for nurturing the bond between you and your child, specially planned, one to one activities add a unique dimension to your relationship.

If you sit down and plan a day out, a half day or evening together you will see a real joy and sense of anticipation build within your relationship as you plan and discuss what you will do together. It is important to build your activity around your child's interests predominantly. This communicates to them in a very tangible way that they are very important to you because you are giving them your undivided focus.

By letting them experience this dedicated focus on them you are showing them how much you value them and how much you like being with them. If you have several kids, space out your father and child times with each one, being careful to spend equal time and money on each one.

Many years ago my accountant said the best thing I could do with my money was to set aside $50 each week so I could spend doing things with my kids. Wow! I never thought I would hear an accountant say something like that! Whilst the $50 did not work in our budget at the time, the principle certainly did. There are many things you can do together that don't cost money, but it is nice to splurge from time to time.

I remember one such father-son date with my eldest son. We went to a golf driving range first and whacked about a thousand balls into the never-never. Then we went to see the latest action movie and finally to round off what had been a terrific time together, we dined like kings at a local Mongolian restaurant. I know he felt extra special that just he and dad were eating out at a great family restaurant.

Finding a way to make a few dollars together through holding a garage sale, selling something door to door, cleaning up a yard could be a valuable part of the whole process together. Teaching your children the value of earning what they later get to enjoy is a valuable lesson in life.

Be creative in the activities you come up with. Ask your child what they would like to do. Ask people at work or in your neighbourhood what things they have done socially with their kids. If you do a computer search for 10 free things to do in your city you will be amazed at what you find. Add to that by searching for fun family activities in your city or town. Be sure to add your father-child date to your diary or wall calendar.

The important thing is to do something regularly and one to one. Your children will never forget the time and effort you made to let them know how important they were to you. Nothing communicates this more loudly than dedicated one to one time doing something special just with them.

I found it easier to take them out of school for the afternoon as it worked better with my schedule at the time. I think it made our dates even sweeter for my boys when I turned up at their school and they got to leave early because they were going out with their dad for a special outing.

I also enjoyed taking my middle son rock climbing recently. He did all the climbing. He is now 19 years old and although we don't get much one to one time these days, I found it to be an equally meaningful time as all those times we had together when he was young.

Some of the unique activities I have enjoyed with him over the years include, drinking bottomless glasses of coke at the Hard Rock Café, visits to Drummers paradise and Billy Hyde's Drum Centre. In more recent times we spent many hours driving far and wide together on his learn to drive permit.

You will need to work around your schedule to make it work of course, but you will be well rewarded by having this devoted one to one time together. Once a term worked for me as I had three sons to schedule. Depending on how many children you have will have a bearing on how many dates you can organize, but at least once per term per child might be a good starting place.

What do you think would work for you?

CHAPTER 2

Build Something

Once you have completed your masterpiece, take some photos to send to relatives, place them on your desk at work or place in your photo album or on your Facebook page. You have bragging rights and when you share with others it helps to reinforce just how proud you are of your child and your combined achievement.

Have you ever stood back and looked at something you constructed and just marveled at your work. Your mind quietly "oohs" and "ahhs" as you admire the lines, the pattern, the contours, the stain or the paintwork. Perhaps the project took days, weeks, or even months, leaving you to wonder if you would ever finish or wondering why you took on such a big project in the first place.

If you are anything like me, then you have. Many a time I have finally finished building a deck, or a path or renovated a bedroom or built the cubby house, then pulled up a chair with a glass of well deserved refreshment in hand, and just sat admiring my work. It satisfies the creative aspect we have within us to sit back and admire our work. There is a sense of accomplishment, a sense of self-fulfillment, when you actually build something. Particularly something that will endure, you hope.

Imagine the mutual sense of satisfaction you and your child or children will share over the years as a result of building something together. To share that deeply satisfying feeling that we built something together is a priceless father-child experience indeed.

We have photos of the first cubby my boys and I built together. It was like a mini house, complete with slide and ladder. It was a beauty. It gave all four of us a great deal of pride that we had built it ourselves. One of my sons and I built a set of bookshelves for his room from some recycled timber. With another I built a driveway from red bricks and we concreted some pathways, with another I landscaped the yard.

The ultimate boys toy we constructed was a Billycart that had a welded brake system and was big enough to seat all four of us with a length of garden hose screwed down along the sides for us all to hang on for our lives. We had hours of fun screaming and laughing our way down the steep road we lived on in Queensland. I'm sure if I had daughters we would have done exactly the same.

The encouragement here is for you to design and build something with all and each of your children. There are some things that you can build as a group. If everyone is going to use it then it makes sense that everyone is involved in the construction.

As in most of this book I am particularly focused on the one to one aspect of your parenting. With each of your children find something that you may like to build together. I suggest something that will be used by the child either in their room or in the yard.

You don't need to build the Taj Mahal or the Great Wall of China. I am talking about building something practical, within your means, and something that you will complete. It may be a practical item that is needed in your child's room such as shelves, a cupboard, a bed, a desk, a doll's house or a wooden train station. It may be a toy, a coloured toy box, a bed head or the repaint of an old rocking horse.

It may be that you build something for outside in the yard like a tree house, a fort, a vegetable garden, a flower garden, a hammock stand, a bike rack, a Billy- cart or a skateboard ramp. Ideally, find something that will be of genuine interest to your child. Something they will use and will last a few years. Design it together, plan it together and build it together. You can Google or You Tube just about anything these days. Sit at the computer together type into the search bar in either of these great tools, how to build a Billy-cart or whatever it is you have decided to construct.

Once you know what you are going to build, decide what materials you will need. Will they be new or recycled? Once you know what you need, make a time together to go buy or collect the materials.

Throughout the building process remember it is more important that you are engaged in building something together. This is more important than the actual project itself. Some of us dads have grown up believing that if you want something done properly do it yourself. If we do this with a stubborn, perfectionist attitude we can guarantee we will finish the project alone. Perfectionists who take over are very hard to tolerate. A second project with your child is not likely to be agreed to. It is all about empowering your child to build something worthwhile with you. Not proving to your child or to others just how good you are at building something.

If you have not been the most practical man about the house, I suggest you build something small and easily achievable to begin with and work your way up the difficulty scale as you gain confidence and, more importantly, skill. Ask your child what they think would be the best way to start, and along the way ask them how they think it would be best to tackle the next stage. As dads we sometimes forget to empower our kids by asking for their opinion or asking them to work out a problem or a strategy. We often take over and just tell them how to do this or that. There is a place for teaching and mentoring for sure, especially on technical skills such as drilling, nailing and using certain tools.

Your child has a brain and they will respect the fact that you ask them for their input before you just dump your knowledge on them or on the project. You may have so much insight and experience, which will be invaluable, but we all need to learn the art of drawing out our child's ability to think, solve problems and construct. It will give them a confidence boost when you ask them what they think first, especially having the safety net of your knowledge and skill as a back up if their suggestion doesn't get the desired results.

Once again we touch on the process of building something worthwhile. This includes making mistakes along the way. Working through our mistakes and persisting are all part of the process.

As previously mentioned, it is very important to finish the project so don't be sucked in to building something too big or grandiose. You may be the sort of person that is very ambitious and idealistic who dreams big dreams. Whilst these are admirable traits, you can sometimes be your own worst enemy when it comes to starting and finishing projects. You will know exactly what I'm talking about here if you are like this. Your wife or partner will certainly point the finger if she is reading this book and knows that her beloved is hard wired this way.

If this is you, you may need to hold back and set about to build something small and make an absolute commitment to complete the project with your child. For all the value in building and completing something with your child, not finishing the project could have an equal opposite effect that is quite destructive for your child.

Demonstrate to your child the value of completing what we set out to build in life. Whether it's a garden bed, doll's house, chook shed, company, business or relationship. You will also have the opportunity to demonstrate patience, persistence, the thrill of learning new skills and teamwork. These are all important life skills you will want to instill in your child's life.

Our children, like us, are experiential learners. Think about what you are modeling for your child as you engage in building something together. Once you have completed your masterpiece, take some photos to send to relatives, place them on your desk at work or place in your photo album or on your Facebook page. You have bragging rights and when you share with others it helps to reinforce just how proud you are of your child and your combined achievement.

Now enjoy what you have built together and from time to time over the coming years mention just how much you enjoyed building it together and how clever you both were to build something as good as that.

CHAPTER 3

Go Somewhere

From reading a range of great fathering books, I was inspired to let my own children know how important they were to me by setting aside this one to one time to go somewhere just with them. It is with great fondness that I remember being alone with my dad standing on the bank of a river as he taught me to tie a hook and sinker on to the fishing line.

He taught me how to thread the wriggly red worm onto the hook so it would stay there during its swim.

My father, Harold, had a deep voice and a large frame. From time to time he sported a grey goatee type beard and moustache. He had a good sense of humour, and he enjoyed making light, jovial conversation with strangers.

I don't recall having much one to one time with him, but the few times I do recall are some of my fondest childhood memories.

I remember catching a huge trout on a fishing trip to lake Eucumbene. Not only was I incredibly thrilled at the luck of the catch, but also my most vivid recollection is of how proud my dad seemed to be of me. He smiled with his trademark cheeky grin.

What is it about being alone somewhere out there with our dad? Is it that we have a longing to explore the wild and dangerous realms of nature? Is it the adrenalin rush when we get to do something a little bit dangerous? Is it the discovery of new territories and the joy of experiencing new activities?

I'm willing to guess that it is a combination of all these things. But from my own experience and the experience of countless other people I have worked with or read about, it is the uniqueness of having had the special time alone with their father, all to themselves.

From reading a range of great fathering books, I was inspired to let my own children know how important they were to me by setting aside this one to one time to go somewhere just with them.

When a dad says to a child, "Son if you and I wanted to go somewhere together for a whole day or for an overnight adventure, where do you think we should go?" You watch the child's eyes light up as the wheels of their imagination go into overdrive. If you said to your daughter, "How would you like to go on a father-daughter adventure, just the two of us?" What do you think her response would be?

When a dad takes their son or daughter on a one to one adventure for a day or a couple of days it communicates a number of messages to the child. It says to the child that I like spending time with you and you are fun to be with. It also communicates that you are enough of a priority in my life that I would put everything else aside just to be with you.

It also demonstrates to your child that they are special and that you value them as an individual person, not just as a member of the family. This is incredibly important in the development of a child's self esteem. I have heard it said that the father has the most significant influence on a child's self image. Obviously a mother has a massive role to play in this as well, but apparently the father takes the lead in this department. A daughter will learn from her father how a girl should be treated. With respect, love and devotion. She needs to know from dad that she is a beautiful princess and deserves to be treated with great love, care and tenderness.

When a father is affirming, admiring, loving and supportive both verbally and physically through spending quality time with their child, boys and girls stand a much higher chance of having a healthier self-perspective and a more positive outlook on life. They will also be more confident and secure in their identity in life as they grow up.

What better way to make this powerful investment in the life of your children than by planning to go somewhere with them?

Naturally you need to communicate with your partner and the other siblings that you want to plan to go somewhere with each of them alone in turn, because another thing we dads need to be is fair and give ourselves equally to each member of our family. Watch out if you don't!

Now that you have decided to go somewhere with one child, the planning begins. The focused one to one time begins when you sit down and plan your escape together. This will build anticipation and give you both something to look forward to together. There is great value in this process in achieving your objectives of communicating how much you value this child.

I recall one of my adventures with the youngest of my three sons. He would have been about seven years of age. We drove about half an hour out of suburbia, parked the car on the side of the road and wandered along an old, disused train line. We decided to make our own bow and arrows and began to hunt for suitable sticks to make arrows and a bigger one each, that would flex enough to make the bows.

In the car I had both string and a pocketknife, so we went back, retrieved these and sat down together carving grooves for the string and sharpening the arrows. We used gum tree leaves in the place of feathers as guides in the almost straight arrows.

It was a thrill to then proceed to shoot our arrows at anything that represented a target. What an adventure for a young boy. In preparing to write this book, I listed as many things that I did with my boys as possible. When I recounted this occasion to my son, he smiled and remembered the time fondly as if it was only yesterday.

We may not get everything right as a dad, I know I haven't, but mark my words when you make the effort to go somewhere with your child and take on some activity or adventure you are certainly making a sound investment in your relationship and in their personal development.

You could go camping, fishing, horse riding, hiking, bike riding, surfing, canoeing, whitewater rafting, sailing, motor bike riding, caving, rock collecting, shell collecting, visit an art and craft market, photography, painting, whatever.

While it is important that you choose activities that you both love to do, it is not so much what you do but that you actually go somewhere together that is important.

Where will you plan to go with your child? What adventures await the two of you? Why not explain to your partner, where appropriate, what you have just read and that you want to take action and begin straight away. Then go and make the invitation. It is probably wise to begin with the eldest child and then tell the other children, where applicable, that they too will each have a turn in the coming months to go somewhere just with you also.

If one of your children needs this attention immediately, perhaps because they have faced a health crisis or have social challenges at school such as bullying or friendship issues or perhaps just need a boost along in their morale, you should make them the priority.

Make sure you explain to each of the other siblings that they will each in turn have this same opportunity and why you are beginning with this particular child. Never underestimate the power of effective communication within the household.

Now go, have the time of their life.

CHAPTER 4

Say Something

The words "I love you" can be hard to say. What are we afraid of and why do these three simple words spend so much time on the shelf? These three simple yet powerful words need to be spoken often and meaningfully to your children.

A well-known biblical proverb says, "The power of life and death are in the tongue." I believe that to be a fact. We can build a person up or destroy a person with the power of our spoken words.

As dads we have an incredible power of influence in our children's lives. Our children hang on every word we speak. If we speak negatively about them we strike a poisonous blow into their being. These negative words can create scars of pain that can cause life-long damage. Often times they will stifle a person's self-belief, also limiting their personal development and their ability to achieve their full potential in life.

Tell your children that you are proud of them. Many have bought the lie that to tell your child you are proud of them will only give them a swelled head. Rubbish! Give them every ounce of encouragement they need and deserve from you. The world will tear them down to size well enough in the years ahead. Be proud of them and let them know it. They need dad to believe in them above everyone else.

Withheld verbal affirmation can also inflict silent arrows of despair, leaving our children wondering whether they ever measured up as good enough in their father's eyes. Words of criticism tear a person down, they are effectively words of death. Many a man and woman carry father-inflicted wounds throughout their lives.

Fortunately for our children, the opposite is also true. When we speak words of encouragement into their lives, they will be built up in their confidence and will have a brighter, more positive outlook on life and the world around them.

Reflect for a moment on the positive words your father spoke into your life. Is it easy to recall them? Are there many or few? How did they make you feel when he spoke them and how do you feel when you recall them all these years on?

Perhaps it is easier for you to recall the harsh or negative words spoken into your life. Perhaps the pain from these is closer to the surface than you thought it might be after all these years. If you haven't spoken with someone about this, my encouragement for you is to take that initiative.

Pain and damage in our lives inevitably cause blockages in our ability to achieve our maximum potential in any area of life, including fatherhood. Whether the pain was inflicted overtly or subtly, the fact remains, the damage is done and we need to work through the pain to find healing.

Where possible, and with the guidance of a skilled life-coach or counsellor, it is best to confront our fathers and work through the process of communication in an attempt to find some form of deeper connection and relationship with them.

It may involve their apology, your own forgiveness toward him and reconciliation at a significant level in your relationship.

You may recall a very powerful song by Mike and the Mechanics, titled "In the living years".

The singer laments that he missed the opportunity for deeper communication with his father when he was alive, and now, since he has passed away, the pain remains and the emptiness lingers. At a recent fatherhood workshop we were facilitating, I was caught off guard when my colleague Wayne played this song for the men attending. I had not heard the song for a while and one of the verses really moved me as it touched a raw nerve that I carry in relation to my own father. Some tears flowed, and while for a moment I was embarrassed, I reminded myself that its good to feel the pain and let it out, so I sobbed quietly in the corner as the melody rolled on.

As I have mentioned, my father died at fifty-five, when I was only twenty-four years of age. Unfortunately I didn't have the opportunity as an adult to go after this reconciliation stuff or to build a man-to-man relationship with him. I like to think we would have had a good relationship. This is one of the deepest areas of loss and regret in my personal life experience. I also remember feeling quite sad that my dad would miss out on meeting our children. Our first son was born eight months after his death. Another time I really wished he had been around was when I was up to my armpits in renovating an entire house and so utterly overwhelmed with the task I had taken on. I just needed him to be there to say, "I am proud of you son, keep going, you are doing a great job!" I wouldn't have minded a bit of a helping hand while he was there as well.

So when I write to encourage other men to go after a deeper relationship with their dads, including tackling the words that were spoken that hurt you or the actions taken that inflicted pain, I am not coming from a theoretical place, I am coming from the reality of my own experience and truly speaking from the heart.

For some this is not possible and I respect that. For those that have a chance, it is still incredibly important to work through the issues as they may be having a limiting effect in your life. Ultimately we all want to fulfill our potential in life, and becoming the best dad we can possibly be is part of that.

I spoke with a friend recently about this very issue and he commented that he enjoys a better relationship with his father now than what he experienced growing up.

I am envious of those men that have great relationships with their dads. I can do nothing about my own. Therefore I am passionate that the men of our generation are encouraged to build quality relationships with their children that will hopefully last a lifetime. This in turn will see them building greater relationships with their children, and ultimately we will begin to break down some of the pain and dysfunction in our world that is caused by under-fathering or a lack of fathering.

Whilst I do believe that these practical fathering steps can make a world of difference in your relationship and your child's wellbeing, it must be said that there are no simple formulas and there are no guarantees how our children will turn out as adults. It sure stacks the odds in the right direction if we have made every effort to be highly effective as dads.

My experience in life to date tells me that life will knock the stuffing out of us one way or another and that there is plenty of negativity out there waiting to smash us down. The schoolyard is a perfect example. Whoever made up the saying that "sticks and stones will break my bones but names will never hurt me" was an absolute liar. I wonder if it was the same person that coined the phrase "Big boys don't cry." Just ask any child that has been teased or bullied. In the workplace, on the sports field, and in other arenas of life, someone will be out to dump a truckload of negativity onto our kids the first chance they get.

Surely we can add to their resilience and preparation by building them up with positive and affirming words, so they are more ready for such adversity.

Phrases like "You make me proud son", "You've got what it takes", "I am so glad you're in my life," "You really are a wonderful daughter", "I am proud to be your dad" or "You did really well today" are powerful deposits into your child's wellbeing. They need the affirmation to be regular and sincere. If you haven't been one to give out much praise and verbal encouragement, now is the time to start.

Your children need to hear you speak these positive uplifting words into their ears and into their life. There are no excuses for not doing this well. Speak positively into the lives of your children! Remember it takes at least 10 positive comments to counter one negative comment. Negative statements do way too much damage in the long run. They are not worth the short-term dagger effect even when we are really tempted to say them. Best to count to ten, cool down and think of another way to do the confronting in such a way as not to inflict lasting wounds in the mind and heart of our child.

One thing to be aware of as a dad is our need to correct our children and give instruction for their improvement. If we give instruction on how to do it better next time or where they could have got a better result each time we give out encouragement, we can negate the positives and our child will only focus on their shortfall. Learn to separate the positive affirmation from needed criticism or suggestions for improvement. Your child can learn to bask in the light of your encouragement without the fear of knowing that dads' lesson on improvement is surely to follow.

Seek to encourage and affirm your child as a stand-alone exercise. At a different time, seek to introduce your perspective on how they might improve their performance in the context of a two-way conversation. Begin the discussion by asking them how they think they went and what they think they could do differently next time that might enhance their performance.

When you are steaming mad, be careful not to direct your anger or frustration at your son or daughter with "you" language. This is very accusing and can be destructive. In contrast, start your statement with "when you do this, I feel"… Then describe how their behaviour or attitude affects you. This is less directed at them and you are less likely to say things you may later regret. They will still get the message loudly and clearly and you will have communicated more effectively.

The words "I love you" can be hard to say. What are we afraid of and why do these three simple words spend so much time on the shelf? These three simple yet powerful words need to be spoken often and meaningfully to your children.

I recently watched a You Tube video where the dad had not spoken the words, "I love you" to his daughter till the day of her wedding. She was twenty-six years of age. In the interview, she claims that she longed for her daddy to say those three simple words. She longed to hear them. She needed to hear them to know that she was beautiful in his eyes. She needed to know that she was valuable to him and, above all, that he loved her.

You want the best for your children. The power of your words, spoken in love and sincerity will have far greater impact on the shape of their life and the person they become than any other aspect of parenthood. This is multiplied when combined with the many other aspects of fatherhood you are reading in this book.

Boys and girls, our sons and daughters, affirmed by their fathers and their mothers in their masculinity or femininity will grow up more secure in their sense of self.

Fatherhood is both an enormous privilege and a massive responsibility. Choose your words wisely and use great words of encouragement as you build the life of your wonderful child, or children.

CHAPTER 5

Model Something

I have heard it spoken by experts that a child's sense of morality, their values, their worldview and their selfperspective are virtually set in concrete by age nine. How important is it to model excellence for our children in their formative years?

An online video search of "children see children do" will both astound you and give you a great laugh. Children mimic the behaviour of those they admire. For many children dad is the hero. Often children idolize their father regardless of how good or bad others may perceive him to be. It is their father they most try to imitate, especially the boys.

A powerful advertisement on television recently captured the importance of modeling responsible adult behaviour. It attempted to dissuade dads from drinking alcohol in front of their sons. It depicted generation after generation of boys becoming men and then drinking beer as a learned and mimicked behaviour after seeing their dads consuming copious amounts of alcohol at every social gathering.

Being an excellent role model is part of being a great dad.

One of the memories I cherish of my dad is the way he spoke with people when we were out and about. He treated shopkeepers and service station attendants as familiar acquaintances. He warmly greeted them, thanked them for their service and he would invariably crack a joke with them, saying something like "you can have the rest of the day off now if you like." They seemed to respond with cheer as he treated them warmly. As a child I took note and it's a learned behaviour that I attribute to my dad. I greet people everywhere as familiar acquaintances, sometimes to their initial surprise. I have even heard myself saying something like "you can have the rest of the day off now, if you like."

I learned from my dad that all people are important and certainly worthy of our warm greeting and brief conversational engagement. Having a laugh with a checkout operator, for example, adds value to their day and shows them that they are important to you as a person, not just as someone that processes and bags your groceries. Being friendly and engaging with people was definitely a quality behaviour that I am glad my father modeled for me.

Hearing people yelling out swear words and abuse from the sidelines at a sporting event makes me want to move seats. Seeing parents model this behaviour for their children makes me shake my head in disappointment at how thoughtless we as parents can be.

The old saying, monkey-see, monkey-do, is as true for children imitating their parents as it is for monkeys imitating other monkeys and humans.

The challenge for us as dads is to make sure that our behaviour and our words are worth imitating. I view this as a positive opportunity to model something of value for our children.

The way we relate to strangers is important as my father modeled for me. This also includes how we answer the phone and how we engage with people we don't know over the phone. Children also listen in on our conversations with family and friends. They subconsciously take note of every interaction we have with others.

How we relate to our children directly will be teaching them how to relate to their children in the future. Of greatest importance is how we relate to our wives or partners. When we hug and cuddle our partner in the kitchen, our children observe that women need to be treated with sincere love, affection and tenderness. When we help our wives prepare the meal or we do the washing up we are demonstrating to our children that the workload needs to be shared by all family members and that mums shouldn't just be expected to do all the work. This includes, washing, ironing, vacuuming and cleaning the toilets. I can hear the mums worldwide shouting "Yes" to that.

When we sit and have relaxed conversation with our partner, our children learn the importance of taking time to connect and re-connect with each other at the end of a busy day. When they observe that we really listen to our wives or partners recount the detail of their day, they see how much we value them and how important it is to show a genuine interest in them and in the events of their day.

Every time we open the door or get a cup of tea for our partners, we demonstrate to our children an attitude of servant-hood toward those we love. Every word of encouragement they hear us speak to our partner shows them that a relationship is all about how we help our partner become everything they were meant to be, whilst demonstrating that we truly believe in them and their potential.

Every time we accept, with gratitude, something our wife or partner has done for us, we are demonstrating that we do not take them for granted. We model our appreciation of them through our thankfulness.

Never underestimate how much our children observe and what messages are being communicated when we relate positively to those people around us. Children's values and behaviours are as much caught, as they are taught.

I have heard it spoken by experts that a child's sense of morality, their values, their worldview and their self-perspective are virtually set in concrete by age nine. How important is it to model excellence for our children in their formative years?

Our attitude to our work, our boss, other women, what we watch on TV, what we listen to and what we pursue as leisure activities all communicate a message to our children. Our attitude to material possessions and money will be observed as well as what we say about the neighbours or about certain relatives on the drive home from the family gathering. Guard our mouths and our behaviour carefully. These are all adding to the shaping of our children's values, behaviours and attitudes.

Remember children see, children do. Seize the opportunity to build depth and quality in your children's lives by modeling quality behaviour and attitudes in every aspect of your life.

CHAPTER 6

Create Something

I'm all for kicking a ball in the backyard and playing cricket or shooting baskets with our kids, the more often the better. However, I wonder how many budding young Picassos are waiting for their creative gift to be ignited by the enthusiasm of an attentive father or mother.

One of my coaching clients had significant artistic skills as a child. He was excellent at drawing. He told me that one day he drew a picture that was so good, his father could not believe that he had drawn it freehand. To prove it, the dad took the piece of artwork to work to show the head designer in the art department.

Upon inspection, the critic decided that a child could not have drawn something so good and that it must have been traced prior to coloring. When Andrew's father returned home that night he was quite angry. He was angry because he believed his son had lied to him and as a result had embarrassed him with his work colleagues. Andrew's artistic talent was squashed there and then by his own father. He had drawn that picture and many like it.

During a coaching session with Andrew, whilst exploring his strengths and attributes, this story came to light. It was clearly an area that held a degree of grief in his life. For many years Andrew did very little drawing. He never pursued something he had been very enthusiastic about as a child because his artistic streak had been crushed by his dad.

I encouraged Andrew to begin drawing with his two sons, aged four and six. He is able to draw perfect replicas of many famous cartoon characters. He reported over the following weeks that his sons thought his artistic ability was amazing. Their eyes would light up as each familiar character appeared magically on a new page simply because daddy was so clever with a pencil or crayon. They sat together for hours while he drew the outlines and they did the colouring.

The three of them enjoyed a new activity together and it gave them a fresh bonding experience. To his delight, his eldest son has begun to show quite an interest in drawing.

I have heard many an adult comment that they don't have a creative bone in their body. I question that. I believe that all people have a degree of creativity within them. They have the ability to create something from the resources around them. True, some are more gifted than others in certain areas, however I personally think that for many, their creative side simply wasn't given the encouragement it needed.

I'm all for kicking a ball in the backyard and playing cricket or shooting baskets with our kids, the more often the better. However, I wonder how many budding young Picassos are waiting for their creative gift to be ignited by the enthusiasm of an attentive father or mother.

The encouragement in this chapter is to get down and create something with our children. We don't need to be great painters or drawers to create something artistic with them. In fact we need very little developed talent at all as there are so many packaged artistic activities available to us these days that it's all there waiting for us. You may, in the process, discover some latent artistic ability of your own. Creativity is therapeutic. It reduces stress and helps stimulate our brain.

Visit any department store or art supply store to discover a world of art and craft bits and pieces for the absolute beginner through to advanced.

There is no dad, with hands intact, that could not do finger painting, or make a paper mache mask on an inflated balloon or melt wax onto paper spelling a child's name or creating an abstract portrait of mum. Blame me if you get into trouble over this last one.

Drawing stick figure cartoons, coloring pictures in a coloring book or creating a small structure from ice-cream sticks and PVA glue are simple places to start. Try melting candles onto toothpicks and joining them together to create a cave or a car or a mini house for a mouse.

How about painting an old faded dolls' house or toy fire station or the dog kennel. Perhaps a couple of the matchbox cars or a model plane need a touch up.

You could create a collage of photos for the wall or a Power Point presentation from a recent family holiday. You could repaint a study desk including flowers or coloured spots or stars, stripes or crazy squiggles. There is no limit to being creative. We are only restricted by our under-developed imagination or the lack of resources at hand. Ask for assistance at the store, letting them know what you are aiming to achieve. Only take on creative activities that are simple and can be done in one hour or less to begin with.

If your child is mature enough, perhaps you would consider creating a model plane together from a hobby store, carefully following the instructions and being meticulous and patient. Perhaps you could buy some balsa wood and cut and glue some other object of interest together.

If you are running short on ideas, use your computer to search for simple craft ideas or easy art to do with children. Remember to decide together what you will create, enjoy the collecting or buying of the necessary bits and pieces and then enjoy the thrill of getting in touch with your creative side together.

Helping your child to develop toward their full potential is what being a great dad is all about. Nurturing their creativity is an important aspect in their development. Creating something together allows you quality bonding time where you will chatter, giggle, make mistakes, laugh some more and from time to time some deeper conversations may flow as a result of taking time to be creative side by side.

The left side of our human brain is the logical side. It deals with facts and figures. This side of our brain helps us to reason and process details and consequences. Our right brain is the creative side. It is with the right side of our brain that we think creatively, see possibilities outside the proverbial square, engage with colour and interact with form and style.

Our children need both the left and right side of the brain to be stimulated for their whole development. Letters and numbers, or literacy and numeracy are vital to grasp so that our children can add, subtract and communicate their way through life.

To fulfill their potential as human beings, our children also need to learn to express themselves artistically. They need to be in touch with their ability to see, feel and communicate non-verbally with the world as well. Your children may develop musically or in the fine arts or they may connect well with dance and movement as their artistic expression. They may combine their literacy skills with their artistic nature and write magnificent poems or songs.

To see ourselves as nurturers of skill and talent in the arts adds another dimension to fatherhood for many of us. Being a dad should be a rich experience for all involved. Creating something together will certainly enrich your relationship with your child as well as nurture their creativity.

If you have access to your children weekly or biweekly, you could plan part of your visit together to involve creating something. Short projects completed in one stay would be recommended initially. As you develop the creative interaction with your child you could take on more complex creations that can be paused between visits. These will provide helpful continuity between visits, giving you both something else to talk about and look forward to when you have midweek contact.

You will have gathered by now that this book is mostly practical, a bit of an action manual for dads. It offers a range of ideas that dads can choose from. Obviously you can't do all of the things written about all of the time or all at once for that matter. Only you can determine which aspects or activities you are able or willing to implement immediately.

I recommend you discuss what you have read with other dads or your partner, the classroom teacher or with your own children. Among them there will be many great ideas, insights and perspectives to add. We can learn from each other. If this book is triggering some new ideas or giving you some fresh perspective and motivation for you as a dad then we are on the right track.

What could you and your child create this week?

CHAPTER 7

Impart Something

You have so much to pass on to your children. Mentoring is about investing yourself in others. It is about imparting something of who you are into the life of another. This chapter is about the transfer of your wisdom into the life of your child so it becomes their wisdom.

Dads have a mentoring role in their child's life. You have had years of experience in life. You will have had some successes and some failures. You would have done some study, read some books and learned many skills. You will have developed wisdom in your paid or voluntary work, you may have become handy around the home or become quite proficient in a sport or other recreational activity. You may have developed excellent communication skills, people skills or business acumen. You may have acquired some expertise in leadership.

You have so much to pass on to your children. Mentoring is about investing yourself in others. It is about imparting something of who you are into the life of another. This chapter is about the transfer of your wisdom into the life of your child so it becomes their wisdom.

When I was a teenager my father was into Permaculture. We had several massive vegetable gardens in our front yard. We had no fence, so our veggies were on display for anyone that passed by.

My dad had read up on how to grow veggies using specific techniques. He was on an invalid pension due to poor health, so I got to do a lot of his spade and barrow work. I enjoyed any opportunity to spend time with my dad. Although I did not work for him for money, I was pleasantly surprised one day when he paid for a new car stereo for my Volkswagen as a thank you for all the work I had done.

He taught me how to establish the raised garden bed and how a thick bed of straw was used, then layers of newspaper followed by a healthy combination of screened top soil, organic compost and animal manure on top. He taught me how to plant which vegetables and at what time of the year to plant them. He grew a lot of veggies. I recall his delight at growing a large species of pumpkin called Big Mac. They grew to one metre in size. I remember dad grinning like a Cheshire cat at the thought of passing neighbours admiring the size of our pumpkins. He was renowned as a big-noter, and loved to impress others any way he could.

In each of our homes I have established vegetable gardens. I currently have a forest of tomato plants. I still plant too many seedlings too close together each time. Otherwise, the wisdom my father imparted to me lives on through my gardening as one example. How I relate to strangers is another. How I tell corny "dad" jokes is another.

My dad also imparted some basic knowledge around fishing, basic home handy-man tasks and most importantly, how to deal with people. He had much wisdom in dealing with people as a result of many years in sales and I am glad of his wisdom in my life and how it has enhanced my ability to relate to others.

I have in turn, passed on to my boys some of my insights gained through the many adventures in my life. Many a time I have found myself attempting to explain things in a mentoring type way, whether its been how to overcome obstacles, dealing with setbacks, setting goals or understanding the different personalities and what makes people tick.

Being a mentor is about being a trusted guide, and the role of mentor within parenthood, I consider to be quite a privilege.

One day on a return trip from a KIDS HOPE speaking engagement interstate, I had a taxi driver ask me what I did for a living. I explained that I worked for World Vision and that my role was to establish a national mentoring program for children in need of additional support. I explained to him that a volunteer mentor spends one hour each week with the mentored child. Together they play games, do schoolwork and the mentor generally seeks to encourage a child within the context of their school day.

He immediately responded "Back in my day they used to be called parents!"

I was stopped in my tracks for a moment, gobsmacked with such a simple, yet confronting statement. How true he was and how disappointing that in a nation as advanced as ours, we have such a massive social, emotional and academic need amongst our children.

As dads we need to step up and be the mentors in our children's lives. Beyond that, if we could spare an hour extra each week perhaps we could each consider becoming a mentor to a child that may not be as fortunate as our own, or someone that just needs more quality input from a caring adult.

Considering that 85 percent of primary school teachers in Australia are female, there is a real need for many more quality men to get involved in our school communities to provide helpful male role models and mentors to Aussie kids. We need to get along side the teachers, most of whom do an excellent job, and offer them our practical support as classroom helpers or mentors. Ask any teacher and they will tell you how many children, especially boys would benefit from some additional input such as the mentoring I have spoken about.

Screened and trained volunteers are welcomed in most schools with open arms.

This could be something you consider as well as being a great dad in your own household. Primarily, our own family and with our own children, is the best place to apply ourselves and hone our mentoring skills before we go helping others.

When imparting something to your children ensure that you pick the right moment. When driving home from a sports training or ballet session you may have the right vibe in the car to impart some of your wisdom. It could be anywhere, but it is often best when it flows as part of a conversation. Asking your child some questions around the subject to firstly see what they do know and secondly, to help them realize that there is a gap in their knowledge to which you may be able to add something of worth.

Be careful to limit your talking to their attention span. If they ask further questions seeking more information from you, their wise sage, consider yourself a genius and indeed a very fortunate dad. The key is to know how much wisdom is appropriate and how much is too much. Know when to talk and when to stop.

I know my wife is going to laugh out loud when she reads this text, as she knows all too well what a chatter-box I am. Even my sons pay out on me for being such a talker. I have had to learn to know when to stop. The occasional elbow from the female passenger in my car has taught me well.

It is sometimes helpful to ask your son or daughter if they would like to know what you think or what you have learned about the situation you are discussing. Always share on an equal level. Not as though you are the expert on all subjects pertaining to life. There is no more certain way to switch your children off from their father's wisdom. You do not want to close the door to future opportunities to be your child's number one mentor of choice because you come across as a "know-it-all."

You have the wisdom and experience to be an invaluable resource to your children. Be sure not to underestimate the value of your input. No one has had all your experiences combined. No one else has lived life through your eyes. No-one else has had your DNA, your family, your upbringing, your personality, and your work and life experience. You are unique. You are a person of great value and as a dad you are a person of tremendous wisdom.

Be available to your child, and the depth of your wisdom will be like a deep well that your children will draw from in the years to come. Continue to learn and grow as a person so that you will always be topping up your knowledge and experience so that your wisdom grows deeper and deeper and the well continues to run mysteriously deep.

I like the notion of life-long learning. Enroll in a new course at night school, embark on a new hobby, a new outlet, or perhaps subscribe to a useful magazine or journal. The more learning you do the wider your conversation range will be and the broader your wisdom will be. Continue to intrigue your children with how much knowledge and wisdom you have.

By doing this, you will forever be a rich asset to your children in the wisdom department, regardless of their level of success and achievement.

Learn how to impart something while they are young. Then steadily through the years impart one small pearl of wisdom after the other, making valuable deposits into their own personal wisdom account.

CHAPTER 8

Be There

If your daughter is into orienteering, show jumping, rock-climbing or dancing or if your son is into football, cricket, snowboarding or shotput you need to be there. If they're keen on surfing, skating, playing guitar in a band or singing in a choir we, as dads need to be there.

It was well after midnight in the middle of winter when my wife and I stood among a small crowd of teenagers and late night revelers in the Gershwin room at the iconic Esplanade Hotel in St Kilda, Melbourne. Being on the other side of forty-five, clearly placed us as the old people on the dance floor.

It would be far more typical that we would be tucked in bed fast asleep at this late hour. However, our middle son was performing with his rock band. He is a keen drummer and we wanted to be there to show our interest in his aspiring musical pursuit. Fortunately for us, they did play great music.

We drove the one hour home and took the next two days to regain our orientation and get our hearing back.

Like so many mums and dads, Karen and I have driven countless miles taking our three sons to sport, school, music lessons and so on. We love watching them play sport and enjoy seeing them involved with a team. One of our sons has played soccer for 15 years and we have seen most of his games. Our other sons have played soccer, inline hockey, ice hockey, baseball and Australian rules footy. We have enjoyed the time spent travelling to games and have felt that sport was an important activity for our sons to learn many important skills and besides, it gave them a chance to burn off some of that teenage energy.

I can vividly recall the highlights, when our middle son scored the winning goal in the hockey final and the team circled the rink to the victory anthem, "We are the Champions". It was a real "Disney moment".

Equally exciting, for us, was when our youngest son kicked his first goal in football. We also felt parental pride when he played baseball and each time he ran around the baseball diamond after hitting the ball.

Seeing our eldest son kick or head goals into the net always gave Karen and I cause for celebration. As a dad, my kids made me proud that they went out there each week and gave their best as part of the team. As parents they gave us so many wonderful moments of enjoyment and have created many family memories.

Sadly, in one of the teams I recall a dad that would come to the games and instead of watching his son playing his heart out, he would sit at a table with his head in a book. I could not believe the height of his ignorance. Didn't he realize how much his son needed him to be watching him, showing a keen interest in his onfield antics? I encouraged him to join me at the fence and watch the game. He replied that he would rather read his book. I am not normally a violent person, but at that moment I sure would have liked to shake some fatherhood sense into his academic brain.

Being there for our kids is one of the most important things we can do as parents. Not being there with our head in a book, or newspaper; but really being there for them, interested, enthusiastic, devoted and cheering.

This past year I have been a first time soccer coach for the under fifteens at Croydon Rangers, my local club. It was a delight to see a handful of very faithful dads attending nearly every game their child played. Regardless of the weather, they were there, coats, gloves, umbrellas and gumboots when necessary. I felt sorry for the boys whose fathers chose not to come and watch their boys play sport on a Saturday morning. Perhaps those that did not choose this option, due to work or other personal commitments, may have found other activities they were able to attend. I would like to think they did.

If your daughter is into orienteering, show jumping, rock-climbing or dancing or if your son is into football, cricket, snowboarding or shotput you need to be there. If they're keen on surfing, skating, playing guitar in a band or singing in a choir we, as dads need to be there.

We may not be able to be at every event, especially if we have several children, but in essence, we need to be there as much as possible for our sons and daughters.

If your son is learning the cello or violin it would be appropriate to quietly sit on the floor and just listen to them practice. Be careful not to wince when they hit a wrong note and it sounds like someone is strangling the cat. Be sure to add an impressed smile or give a thumbs up now and then to indicate how well you think they are doing. You only need to sit there for 10 minutes and then later on make a brief comment about how well they are coming along with their instrument.

Never underestimate how much your child will appreciate that their dad takes the time to sit down and show a genuine interest in what they are doing. This is being there for them. It doesn't require a lot of time or effort, but it does send a very loud message to your child. They need to know that their dad is interested in them and what they are doing. It boosts their confidence when dad notices them and when he affirms them in what they are doing.

As mentioned, I have one son who plays the drums. It was my pleasure as his dad to slip into his room or the music room and just park myself unannounced on the floor and just marvel at his drumming skills for 15-20 minutes, give him an affirming nod, show him that I was genuinely impressed and quietly leave again. I would do this perhaps every two or three weeks. He could not help but break out with a big smile when he got the thumbs up from dad after a brilliant new drum roll sequence. Being a great dad is a matter of being more aware, looking for opportunities for connection and actually putting what we know into action. Often it's the little things done consistently over a period of time that makes the significant difference in our children's lives.

My youngest son is a guitarist. Being a more private person, he was not so fond of performing for others, so it was a lucky day when I could cruise in and just listen to him playing. He has great skill on the guitar and I enjoyed listening to him play. However I had to be sensitive that he liked his solitude time and that he did not necessarily thrive on having an audience. So needless to say as dads we need to be sensitive to each child and their space.

Once again the earlier in their life we begin being there for them the more natural it will become for them and having dad around and involved in their lives will be the norm. Your children will want you around lots when they are young.

Be warned however, there will come a time when most kids will go through a phase where they push away from mum and dad and everything adult, as they journey toward their own adult self. Our children make certain decisions or display various attitudes toward us that we don't like. This is quite normal, albeit quite horrible as well.

The more you are there for your children as they are growing up, the greater the chance they will welcome having you involved in their world during their teen years. The more you have been there for them throughout their childhood and adolescence the more likely they will feel a strong connection with you in their adult lives.

Remember there are no guarantees. Most of us older dads have experienced levels of heartaches, occasional disappointment and pain from our kids at times.

And naturally, there are no guarantees how our children will choose to live their lives when they get older. There are no concrete formulas that ensure the outcomes we want or think would be best for them. As they strive for independence, some will completely throw off everything that we represent.

One thing I know I have looked forward to as my children were growing up was to enjoy quality relationships with them when they themselves became men.

As I write this book, my boys are in the transitioning years of preparing to leave our home. We are not entirely sure when the nest will be empty. Apparently the average age of home leavers is now 25.

I feel that I have applied what I am now writing about and believe

I have made a reasonable investment in their development and our relationships. I know there are areas I could have done better and things I wish I had done more of.

Maybe one day I will write a sequel and give an update on our relationship and what it's like to have adult child-to-father relationships. I look forward to that. Especially when grandkids come along. In fact I like the connotation of being a Grand Father.

Take the encouragement to be there for your kids. Whatever it costs, however difficult it may be, find a way to be there for them. As I wrote in one blog, what could possibly be more important than being there for our kids.

CHAPTER 9

Share Something

It was a vulnerable moment. I took the opportunity to tell my son that I had made mistakes in my life and have needed to learn from them.

It was a clear night as we lay on the trampoline looking up at the stars. My son and I were having a very confronting conversation. He was 14 and I had just given him a serious talking to. His behaviour had been way less than acceptable in certain areas and it was having a very negative effect on our family life.

I took him for a walk and told him that his behaviour was causing grief within our home life and that it needed to come to an immediate halt, otherwise we would need to take serious action. I gave him some background of how we have faced some real uphill battles to raise a family, mostly due to illness and the enduring financial challenges that went with that. I explained that we have placed the importance of having a quality family life over every other priority. I explained that we valued our three boys and our family unit more than anything else in life.

Against this backdrop, I confronted the changes he needed to make in both his behaviour and his attitude. With tears welling in my eyes, the truth needed to be told. I found the tough love stuff to be unfamiliar territory for me. It was not something I thought I would have experienced in our household, certainly not at this level of seriousness.

It goes to show that you can do your very best at being parents but there are no guarantees as to how your children are going to behave and as many before us have experienced, the teenage years can turn your little darlings into horrible monsters. I once heard a mother speaking at a conference about her teenage sons. She commented that she wished we could legally put her children into the freezer for three years and get them out when they were nice again.

My son got the picture and, perhaps for the first time, he really grasped just how important a family unit was and what price has been paid for him to belong to one. He made a significant apology and promised to change, starting immediately.

It was a vulnerable moment. I took the opportunity to tell my son that I had made mistakes in my life and have needed to learn from them.

I told him that I had to make whatever changes were necessary at the time, apologize to others where needed, and then move on.

My father had also shared with me that he had made plenty of mistakes in his life. He said that if he had learned something from all these mistakes, he would be a very wise man by now. Spoken at age 50.

When the right moment presents itself, I believe it is constructive to share something of your weaker self with your child. Comments such as " I failed at that", or "my first business venture fell flat", or "I made a bad choice on an investment", or "I wasn't very good at such and such" can broaden your child's perspective on who you are.

You need to say whatever is useful and relevant in the context of the actual moment. There are certain weaknesses or failings that are inappropriate to share with our children, you will need to use wisdom in knowing what to share and what to hold back. It is constructive for them to know you are real, that you are human and that you do make mistakes. I am a strong believer in being authentic in our relationships.

It is also important to explain what action you took to resolve the past situation and tell them what you learned from your mistake. This openness from a dad creates a powerful life lesson for your child.

During the teenage years there will be many confrontations in most homes, and hopefully these will create opportunities for deep and meaningful conversations.

Immediately following these confrontations, there may be brief vulnerable moments between you. They tend not to last very long, so on occasion, make the most of them by giving your child a glimpse into the weaker side of who you are as a person, or who you have been in the past, if it seems appropriate to do so. Nobody is perfect and everybody has made mistakes. It is how we grow as a person and how we learn some of life's most important lessons that matter.

Failures are but a stepping-stone to our successes. Every child needs to learn that failing in life is a natural part of getting things right and moving forward. Who better to teach them this valuable life-lesson than their own dad?

Being open and transparent in this way will help to shape your child's view of you more broadly. It also teaches them, by example, how to communicate on the more tender subjects in life.

There will be times, naturally, following a verbal altercation that you are both angry and have marched off in different directions. In these times wait till the heat has reduced, and in your cooled down state apologize where necessary and then see if a tender moment presents itself for some sharing of your self.

You need not wait for such a time of conflict to share something of your self. There may be times when your son or daughter will come home from school carrying the weight of the world on their shoulders. Perhaps they were not chosen for the dance group or the soccer team. Perhaps they got in trouble or didn't do so well in a test or a presentation. Worse still, they may have been bullied or teased at school.

These are times when your child is open and quite vulnerable. They need reassuring from both their parents. If dads can come alongside their child in a supportive way, there is often an open window for meaningful connection between father and child. Seize this opportunity to make that personal connection. Take the moment to reflect with your child a similar experience that you may have had either as a child, teen or as an adult. A time when you felt left out, lonely, afraid or hard done by. Acknowledge that it was painful and that it hurt for you.

At first your child will be surprised to hear that their dad had some tough times emotionally. It will again give them a fuller perspective of you and your life and ultimately a deeper appreciation for you as a person, with feelings. It will also teach the importance of sharing your feelings and vulnerabilities.

Just as important is the fact that your child will receive the comfort of their compassionate father and they will find strength in relating their experience to yours. With a few encouraging words and a big hug, hopefully your son or daughter will have renewed courage to face the next day and gradually, over time will develop inner resilience to the bumps and bruises that life will cause along the way.

Aren't you glad to be a dad? You have so much influence in your child's life. Your role as a dad must never be underestimated or devalued. You have the privilege of shaping their life. Take every opportunity to share something from your own life experience, be they good or bad experiences. Your child wants to know your story. Think about your story and how you can best relate it to your child. Then build on these by adding value to the conversation with affirming, encouraging and uplifting words spoken with love into your child's life.

They will be bigger, stronger and more confident as adults because you took the time to share something of yourself as they were growing up.

You contribute to being a life shaper. Put into practice what you are reading. Seek to be an emotionally connected dad. This will not only boost your child in their life, but it will add strength to your life-long relationship with each other. Be open and ready to share something.

Avoid the trap of being a closed book, depriving your loved ones of the real you.

What does it mean for you to be authentic in your relationships?

Was your father open emotionally or was he a closed book?

If this is unfamiliar territory for you, you are not alone. Small steps in the right direction can be taken.

What one step could you make today with your children.

CHAPTER 10

Read Something

When a child is behind academically at the beginning of their education they can spend the rest of their school life playing catch up. Often branded as dumb and stupid by the other children and sometimes, sadly, even teachers.

During the establishment phase of the KIDS HOPE AUS mentoring program in Australia, I heard so many teachers say that reading with the child would be one of the most valuable aspects of the mentoring hour.

The teachers knew that if a child would develop a love for reading, their potential to learn was limitless. Seven years later some 10,000 children have benefitted from having a personal mentor for at least one year of their schooling. Many have had the same KIDS HOPE mentor for their entire primary schooling years. They have contributed thousands of hours of reading time with these children.

The first child I mentored was five years of age. It was well into the academic year and his teacher explained that he could only identify 14 letters of the alphabet and had no reading ability at all. He was clearly well behind the rest of the class academically and socially. The teacher had identified him as being at risk of lagging behind the rest of his peers.

She knew from past experience that this would have a negative bearing on his social relationships and in turn would affect his personal esteem and as a consequence, his behaviour would become more attention-seeking as a way to compensate. How common this scenario is in the lives of many children. It could be prevented if we as dads learned to sit down and read something with our children every night if possible as part of our overall involvement in their lives.

My KIDS HOPE story is not unique, but it is heartwarming and well worth telling.

Timmy (not his real name) and I spent two years together as mentor and mentee. We did puzzles, kicked a football, bounced a basketball and had running races in the courtyard. Inside we drew pictures and coloured in, we did number puzzles and we read books. It was simple. It was regular and it was fun. He seemed to look forward to my visit to the school as much as I looked forward to meeting with him. Having had three sons of my own, I had a fair idea how to relate to a boy.

After the initial eight weeks, his mother came to the school to meet and thank the person who had made such a difference in her child's life (her words). She joined us for the entire mentoring hour. I will never forget her delight as Timmy correctly identified every letter in the alphabet. He then proceeded to read his entire take-home reader, only needing slight prompting with two of the words. She beamed at her child's success. He was visibly pleased with himself as well.

His teacher later told me that Timmy had become so much more confident and now participated in class discussions as well as taking a keen interest in drawing and colouring accurately, an activity he had not shown any interest in previously.

It was hard to believe that just one hour per week of personalized one to one attention would make such a difference in a child's life. This was confirmed at the end of the year when the teacher wrote in Timmy's report that he had become a very confident class member and was now reading at grade level. She wrote in the report that this positive development was directly attributable to spending time with his KIDS HOPE mentor.

Were his parents bad parents? I don't believe so. They were just so incredibly busy running a business that their children did not get much time with them. Dad would work 6 days a week 6am till 10pm every day. There was no time or energy to even think about the development of his children. Being clothed, fed and taken to school each day was all their parents could manage.

Timmy's development is a good example of how a child does not develop when dad or mum are not able, or simply choose not to spend important and valuable time with their child. Initially I read books to Timmy. Gradually, as his confidence grew, he began to read small portions out loud to me. We read together and eventually he was reading by himself. This reading, as part of our hour together each week, became pivotal in his transformation as he grew in confidence and began to play catch up with the rest of his class.

It was exciting to hear him reading most of a book by himself.

When a child is behind academically at the beginning of their education they can spend the rest of their school life playing catch up. Often branded as dumb and stupid by the other children and sometimes, sadly, even teachers.

Naturally this affects children in their social and emotional development as well their academic development, often compounding into social misbehaviour such as the bullying of other children, class room disruption and can translate into community delinquency, gang activity, drug abuse and law breaking in years to come.

Whilst this all sounds rather dramatic, the evidence is there to support the fact that we need to be reading to our children. As a case in point, the government department responsible for the prison system, in both California and Indiana in the USA, can predict with accuracy how many beds in prison they will need 10-15 years from today based on their current grade-three reading averages across the state. A frightening thought.

Back to you and your household. How much time do you spend reading to, and with your child, or children?

Reading picture books to begin with then gradually progressing through the years to basic novels and special interest books, and then progressing to bigger novels and specialized books that may be about science subjects, horses or dogs or planes for example.

At a weekend family retreat a few weeks ago, one dad told me that his teenage kids still like him reading to them, even tackling a book as big as Harry Potter. He set the pattern early and his kids still love to have him read to them. By the way they can all read very well for themselves.

Your children love the tone of your voice, the way you spice up the story with funny voiceovers and your unique voice inflections. Younger children enjoy snuggling up to you and can feel the vibration of your voice through your chest as well as listening to your familiar voice. If you have not read to your children and they are now teenagers, it is difficult trying to introduce reading to them.

Perhaps comics or special interest magazines may be a place to start.

There may be a book they are wading through for school and finding it hard going or onerous. You could suggest that you read a chapter out for them. Who knows, they may ask you to read another. Now wouldn't that be a nice discovery.

For dads with younger children, tonight is the ideal time to create a new habit in your home. Be sure to read to each child individually as well as when the whole family is together. Include all the family in the love of books and see if you can make it a daily essential ingredient in the recipe of building academically successful children in your home.

Mums often do most of the reading with children and we don't want to replace this. We want to add to this. Be sure to wait in turn to read for your kids if mum has been the main reader. You don't want to compete with your partner or set yourself up as the knight in shining armour arriving at this late stage to rescue your kids.

Just casually suggest that you would like to read a few pages after mum has read to the kids. Be sure to encourage your partner with all that they have done in investing in your children. Explain to them, if you haven't been involved in this side of things to date, that the book you are reading has helped you see the importance of getting more involved in your child's development and that reading would be a good place to start.

CHAPTER 11

Write Something

A sure-fire way to capture your thoughts and express them meaningfully to your son or daughter is to write a personal letter and post it to them. I suggest you set aside a block of at least 30 minutes. It could be your lunch break today.

While attending a KIDS HOPE USA leadership conference in Michigan, I heard a remarkable story told by one of the speakers. It is a very telling account of the influence of fathers in the lives of sons.

A Hallmark greeting card executive had a generous idea. He made available to the major prison in his home state enough mothers' day greeting cards for every prisoner to be able to send one home if he wanted to. The result was considered a huge success in that all of the cards were taken and sent to mothers far and wide. It was a real morale booster both in the prison and back at Hallmark head office.

Several months later Fathers' day approached. The executive thought it to be an equally generous gesture to make the same amount of cards available for the inmates to be able to write home to their dads.

What amazed all those involved, was what happened. Nothing. Not one fathers' day card was selected from the display tables and not one was sent home to any dad from any of the prisoners.

It was staggering. The executive was not so much disappointed that the greeting cards had not been used, but rather that not one prisoner had enough relationship with their father worthy of a special fathers' day greeting.

It makes me wonder about all male inmates across the world and beckons the question; what if they had had a great relationship with an emotionally connected and involved father? Would they be behind bars today? How would their life journey have been different?

A school principal recently reported to me that Dr. Bruce Robinson from Perth, Australia, a researcher into child development, reported at a conference for School Principals held in Melbourne recently, that from his extensive research into the development of children, the father figure has the single greatest influence in a child's growth as a person. This included emotional and social wellbeing as well as academic achievement. A profound insight when we know that it is mostly the mothers that carry the bulk load of raising children in our culture.

This is a big call, and when I can access his research I would like to read it.

If this is true, and I have no reason to doubt his research, we need to hear and respond to this bold claim, starting today. Each of us needs to be more intentional about our involvement in our children's lives. That is the absolute essence of this book.

The many practical things I have written about are foundational. You may have a list of proactive parenting suggestions. These are welcome at my website (via editing), www.gooddadsgreatdads.com

One way we can boost our children's sense of personal value is by writing something meaningful to them. While I think emails do not seem as personal as a card or letter, they are a good place to start, especially if you spend hours in front of a computer away from your kids. Letting your daughter or son know that you are thinking of them and that you are looking forward to catching up with them when you get home from work will mean a great deal to them.

The fact that you even took the time to send an email may give them a surprise.

The next step in writing something to them is to venture down to a local shop that sells greeting cards. Look for a card that best represents your child and their interest or hobbies or in some way reflects your relationship with them.

Take it back to your desk and write a personal note to them. Things you could write about could be; the qualities you admire about their personality or some attribute of their character that stands out to you. You could tell them how proud you are of them just because they are who they are, or perhaps because they have achieved some special goal that was important to them.

Often we can express ourselves better when we sit down with a pen and paper than when we try to say what we're thinking. This doesn't excuse us from trying to express ourselves face to face. There is a whole chapter on the importance of spoken communication. But for now it is important to understand how powerful your written words are in your child's life.

Most girls are quite sentimental about special things others have given to them. An item as personal as a card that you, her very own dad, took time to write will be a treasured keepsake for years to come. She will probably read it time and time again. And whilst boys are generally not so sentimental you can bet they will take your kind and thoughtful words to heart. It may be a treasured item in the room for a few days or even weeks until it gets lost in the mess.

Every now and then drop a brief note into your child's lunch box telling them that you love them and you hope they have a great day. You may write that you are looking forward to seeing them after work or encourage them to go well in their exam, music performance or sports competition. Just the very fact that you demonstrate that you are thinking about them will add to their sense of personal value. My dad cares deeply for me. How many lives would turn out so very differently if dads everywhere started to show more thought and communicated more to their kids.

Our children's development is not something we can take for granted. We cannot simply leave it to their mother or their school teachers. Our input is a vital part of the process.

On that note, how many marriages or relationships would improve dramatically if us blokes took the initiative to communicate our thoughts and feelings to our partners more often and more creatively.

A sure-fire way to capture your thoughts and express them meaningfully to your son or daughter is to write a personal letter and post it to them. I suggest you set aside a block of at least 30 minutes. It could be your lunch break today.

Choosing an appropriate piece of paper that you have hand selected, begin to write your letter of love and affirmation to your child. It's ok to say you haven't done this before but felt that it was high time you did.

Reflect on some of the highlights from the past, some of the ways this child has brought joy to you and your household. Itemize their qualities as you see them.

Affirm them for the contribution they make to the family and the running of the home. Admire them for their personal achievements and more importantly for their qualities of character. Tell them of the feelings you have for them. For example, the pride you take in her or the happiness he adds to your life. Tell them how much you love just hanging out with them and the way they have made your experience of fatherhood be more than you could ever have expected.

Speak about their sense of humour or their laughter, their smile or their dress sense or their artistic ability. You could mention their abilities in craft, sport, the way they care for their siblings or the neighbour's kids. You might mention how much they support their mother or how they help you in the garden.

Sound mushy? Good. This is not a letter to your CEO and is not for anyone else's eyes except that of your son or daughter. Think on this: how much do you wish your father had communicated more of his feelings to you? No more squirming. Just do it!

Round off the letter by looking forward. Write about what you are looking forward to in the future. It could be their life pursuits, the next family holiday, their graduation, a hike that you two are planning, or them finding a very special partner in life that will look after them totally. Whatever it is, let them know that your love and admiration for them is for yesterday, today, tomorrow and always.

If you are a typical male, as I am, it is easy to forget doing such things as writing notes or cards or sending a letter. I recommend that you jot something in your diary at regular intervals to remind you to take action. Good intentions get you nowhere in your relationship with your kids and they certainly don't assist your child to get the boost in life they need to be emotionally and socially strong.

Give your child every chance to succeed in life by being a communicating father. I wonder what you might want to write?

CHAPTER 12

Pray Something

It is not my intention here to discuss theology or differing beliefs. I am writing to those for whom this aspect of life is relevant and they would like to know how to be more effective in nurturing their child's spiritual nature.

A father over heard his child saying a prayer. "Dear God, please help me to be like my daddy." Later that evening the man prayed, "Dear Lord, please help me to be the sort of dad my son wants me to be."

Many people do not believe in prayer or give much attention to the spiritual side of life. I respect that and I respect you if this includes you. Statistics tell us that most people have a belief in the divine in one form or another. So going with a majority, I chose to address this area of life. Your personal beliefs are respected, as I trust, with you, so are mine.

It is not my intention here to discuss theology or differing beliefs. I am writing to those for whom this aspect of life is relevant and they would like to know how to be more effective in nurturing their child's spiritual nature.

I do believe in prayer and I believed in praying with my children as they were growing up. I still pray for my grown children and while I may not be the most devout pray-er, I do have a faith and have found great strength and guidance over the years through prayer.

If you are a praying man, then take time to pray for help in being the best dad you can be. Pray for your children regularly. Pray about their future. Pray about the choices they will make in life. Pray for their protection and guidance.

Each night, as part of the bedtime routine, I prayed with my boys. When they were young and shared a room, I prayed for each of them by name, thanking God for each one. I acknowledged His provision of our health and our daily needs and I entrusted family decisions and our future into His hands. As they grew older and had separate rooms I took time to visit with each one, read a story, have a little chat and then conclude with a bedtime prayer. I particularly enjoyed these one to one times together.

I wanted to teach my boys that I was grateful to God and that the spiritual part of our lives was an important aspect that needed daily attention.

Sometimes one of the boys would say a prayer, which would cause my wife and I to smile, but most often it was up to Karen or I to say the prayer. In some households I'm sure that children can be quite chatty in prayer. It wasn't the case in our home.

Each evening a prayer of thanks would be spoken at the dinner table. We would often pray about the needs of someone we knew or pray for people in other countries that did not have food or water, asking God to provide for them and to help us do what we could to help others in need as well.

It will be interesting to see as life unfolds what effect this praying together with our children will have in shaping their beliefs and experiences. In many non-western countries spirituality is as natural a part of life as eating and sleeping.

In our western culture spirituality is observed as an optional extra, neglected by many until life is threatened or tragedy strikes.

I don't buy into religious formulas, self-centred, quick fix or trendy spirituality. I do buy into a life where we give the spiritual dimension the attention it needs. As with many aspects of life, in which we as men may stumble forward, feel awkward or perhaps nervously "wing it", we would do well to feed our spirit and nurture the spiritual dimension in our children's lives.

There are many books written on this subject and indeed there will be many references on the web awaiting you and your search engine to find them. I encourage you to discuss spirituality with others to hear what they do regarding the spiritual nurture of children.

My aim here has been to stimulate your thinking, not provide the "one size fits all" approach to nurturing spirituality in our young. May you embark on some research and become more conscious of fostering healthy spirituality in your children's overall development.

Some of the aspects of prayer I have covered in raising my own children may well relate to your own situation. No doubt there will be more. Whole books have been written on the how to, and it is not my intention to begin to compete with them but rather to guide people to them for their own discovery and learning.

The wheel of life is a coaching tool used by coaches with their clients. It is a way to look at each segment of life and view this aspect of life in the context of the whole. Spirituality forms one segment of the wheel. Like the other segments, it is also an important segment within the overall structure and balance of a person's life. There is an interconnection between each and every segment of our life. The same is true for our children.

You may like to work through this tool by yourself or get some coaching support to assess your overall life balance and to determine how aligned things are for you. Do a computer search for "wheel of life" diagnostic or assessment tool.

The spiritual dimension was not included in my own upbringing but became an area of importance to me in my late teens and continues to this day. I have chosen not to go into a lot of detail but will gently prompt you to take on board the encouragement offered in this brief but important chapter.

CHAPTER 13

Why do children have different personalities?

To help you understand why each of your children behave so uniquely and how you can better understand them and relate more effectively with them, we will look at different personality types.

Why are some children neat, tidy and organized? Why do some children sit quietly for hours content to draw or play with building blocks while other children scream around the yard covered in mud chasing the dog all day?

Why do some children need to perform concerts every night or whenever visitors come over? Why do some children save their money meticulously and others squander every cent as soon as possible? Why do some fuss over the way they look and others don't give their personal presentation much thought?

Why are some teenager's bedrooms spotless and ordered, while the rooms of others always look like a hurricane has just passed through?

To help you understand why each of your children behave so uniquely and how you can better understand them and relate more effectively with them, we will look at different personality types.

In describing the personality types I will talk about people in general terms with some specific detail about children. As adults we need to grasp this material as it relates to ourselves and to those around us in all contexts. As we grasp this in relation to our peers, we can then apply the knowledge to understanding the differences in children.

Hippocrates, the great Physician and Philosopher, who lived 400 years before Christ, determined from his observations that there were four basic personality types. The Choleric, the Sanguine, the Melancholy and the Phlegmatic.

In our modern world there are many interpretations of these four personalities. Some of you will be familiar with Myers Briggs, D.I.S.K or Personality Plus. I am a fan of the book Personality Plus by Florence Littauer and I have recommended it to many of my clients over the past 18 years.

In a household there will be any number of personality types living together. Similarly, you will find many different personalities in your place of work or in your community or sportsgroup. When you understand your own personality better and what makes you tick, and also understand the personalities of those around you, you become more understanding and tolerant and more effective in your overall relationship with them.

I will briefly describe each of the four personalities with both adults and children in mind. Then I will apply this information specifically to children with some examples how to use this information to better communicate and connect with your children according to their personality type. I have found that when we understand the different personality types and what drives them, we have a far greater chance of connecting well with people according to their nature and way of operating, including our children.

In my coaching work with executives and managers, this is always an important ingredient covered to increase their relational effectiveness with their staff. Having the basic understanding of temperaments, as they are also referred to, will also help you understand your partner better and the other people that are part of your life.

Grasping this knowledge is pivotal to improving your relational or people skills.

Taking a small amount of time to invest in this knowledge can help you know how better to relate to your children according to their personality type.

Whenever I speak on the four personalities or run a workshop on them, they seem to generate the most excitement and enthusiasm as the information clicks for participants. It is as if the lights go on in understanding why we all act and behave the way we do. Many a relationship has been saved from ruin by the discovery of the different personalities and how we can complement each other.

I remember when I first learned about the different personality types. It was a huge eye opener for me.

The Choleric

"My Way or the Highway!"

The Choleric person is usually the strongest and dominant type person. They are usually decisive, action or task oriented, extroverted and often opinionated. They often end up in CEO, Senior Management, School Principal, business founders or hospital Matron type roles.

Choleric people often end up leading others because they like to be in control and they like to get the job done.

Choleric people can step on toes, ruffle feathers, but this does not matter so much to them, as long as the job gets done. Their dress code is mostly conservative and always practical. They prefer neatness, tidiness and order, because they do not like wasting time working through mess and after all, "Cleanliness is next to godliness!" and "Time is money!"

A child exhibiting "bossy britches" behavior may well be showing their choleric traits early. Choleric people like the facts and the bottom line so it is important to get to the point with a Choleric. They like to know what is in it for them, or what the outcomes will be. They don't like time wasting and "beating around the bush".

The Choleric person is usually very results driven. It benefits the Choleric greatly to develop the "soft skills" in dealing with people. When they learn the art of respecting other people and their feelings and learn to relate more sensitively to others, Choleric people are dynamite. They are world shapers, history makers, pioneers of industry and social development. They get the job done at any cost.

The Sanguine

"Give me a microphone and a spotlight please."

The Sanguine person often adds life and sparkle to the party. They are the most extroverted of the personalities. The room seems to light up when the Sanguine walks in. They are usually chirpy, singing or laughing. When there is a loud ruckus down the corridor you will often find a Sanguine person telling jokes or colourfully descriptive stories to a group of enthralled listeners. They find "water cooler conversations" and lunchtime catch-ups the most stimulating aspect of going to work. They thrive on people contact, like to be interrupted from their task if it means people contact. They welcome phone calls and face-toface meetings far above email communication.

Sanguine people are very spontaneous. They will often be the first to volunteer for Karaoke, to make a "thank you" speech or respond when a group is asked, "are there any questions?" The Sanguine person tends to do their thinking while their mouth is speaking. They process their thoughts while the words are forming on their tongue. The technical term is verbal processor.

People that have a Sanguine temperament usually gravitate to jobs involving lots of people contact. They often end up in sales, product promotion, public speaking, drama, theatrical and acting type engagements. They love the stage and putting on a performance.

Often Sanguine people have great ideas and can be quite idealistic, thinking that every idea is a winner and that the results are assured. They love to start new projects; especially with others they have enthused to join them. Completing things can be a challenge for the Sanguine as the next exciting thing easily gets their attention.

Sanguine children love having fun. The fun factor is essential if you want to persuade a Sanguine person to get involved.. Their rooms will often be messy, but always colorful. "Hey dad, can we paint my room four really bright colors, one for each wall and could we put sparkles that glow in the dark on the ceiling? Mmm? Pleeeeeeaaaaase, c'mon dad, it will be fun!"

They love to put on a concert for the family demonstrating their singing, dancing or acting skills. "Ladies and gentlemen welcome to my show!"

The world is a brighter place thanks to the many Sanguine personalities that entertain us as singers, movie stars, stage actors or street performers and party-goers.

The Melancholy

"Mmmm, let me think about that."

The Melancholy personality is the attention to detail, perfectionist and the deep-thinker type. They love to analyze things before they make a decision or a comment. They are reflective, sensitive and introverted. They can get "peopled out" before the other personalities and need to be re-energized by spending time alone. They like to process all the possible outcomes, the "what if's" and the "what abouts?"

The Melancholy person likes graphs, charts and sequences. They are more planned than spontaneous. They like to have calculated the detail before they embark on any mission, venture or activity.

The Melancholy likes everything to be in its place and to ensure there is a place for everything. Neatness is crucial to their personal sanity. They are very creative people and the world has benefitted from many brilliant melancholic people that have become the greatest chefs, cake decorators, songwriters, composers, poets, painters, sculptors, writers, architects and playwrights.

116

Because melancholy people are such internal thinkers, they need time to process information if you want them to contribute their thoughts. These will be well thought out responses that may be accompanied with a graph or a chart to demonstrate possible outcomes, costings and risks.

They can tend toward having more "dark cloud" days than others. They are sensitive and tend to be more in touch with their feelings. To the Melancholy person, quality is more important than quantity and this can be reflected in friendships. They make very reliable, faithful and life-long friends with a small group of select individuals rather than have a stream of people flowing through their life. This is important to note when you observe your children's friendship selection.

The melancholy child will be sensitive, reflective and thoughtful. They need to be treated in such a way as to respect these traits. It is quite natural for them to appear more introspective than the other temperaments, keeping their thoughts or feelings to themselves. When they have had time to process their thoughts they may be ready to share these with you, but you will need to extract these through private one to one conversations rather than at the dinner table with everyone gathered.

They will usually be ordered and neat, sometimes meticulous. This is how they like things. Play accordingly with their approach to games and puzzles. Following the rules closely and being fair are important to a melancholy child. They are more than likely to be creative so making sure you connect with them through creative activity. This will add to your relationship.

The Phlegmatic

"We'll just wait and see what happens, no pressure."

The easy going, laid back and carefree individual. Ah, the seemingly stress free life of a Phlegmatic. Nothing seems to fluster them. At times they can appear to be so casual and nonchalant. They are very content to be in the background, not needing any of the limelight.

The Phlegmatic is often the bearer of very witty jokes or wise cracks, often seeing the funny side to more serious situations. They can make great comedians because of their skills in observation, timing and delivery. They tend to have a dry sense of humor and are often very endearing because of their ability to deliver perfectly timed one-liners with a deadpan, expressionless face. The phlegmatic personality can seem so relaxed or non-enthusiastic. I once heard a Phlegmatic presenter claiming that the reason he is so relaxed is that he conserves his energy in case of an emergency.

The Phlegmatic person is usually not so bothered by their appearance, if their clothes aren't the latest fashion but they do the job, that's fine. If their hair is a little out of place, they are not so fussed. If the car is unwashed or untidy and there are clothes left on the floor or the desk is cluttered or dusty, chances are a Phlegmatic person lives here.

Some of the qualities of the phlegmatic person are that they have stick-ability. They will stay with a project until completion, even if there is no rush to the finish line. They make very reliable and trustworthy friends. They are good listeners and are easy to talk with. Their easygoing nature helps to keep perspective on stressful situations. They help to balance out the seemingly manic and sometimes highly strung approaches to life of the other temperaments.

While many Sanguine and Choleric types steal the centre of stage in their upfront roles and gain most of the notoriety for their public achievements, it's often the Phlegmatic who quietly works behind the scenes to ensure that all the really important, but less public things, get done. They are very reliable people to have on your team.

The phlegmatic child will be relaxed and quite stress free. They can be so easy going that they may appear to be lazy and unmotivated. This can be quite frustrating for a father or mother of a choleric nature who, as I have said, are more task, activity and achievement oriented. There are sports and activities that phlegmatic children prefer. These tend to be the less excertive options. Consider this when suggesting things to do with your phlegmatic child.

Personality Combinations

It is important to understand that we each will have traits of the other personalities. For example you may be predominantly Choleric, with strong Melancholy or Sanguine traits as well. You may be predominantly Phlegmatic, but have some fairly strong aspects of the Sanguine or Melancholy personality.

Depending what your context is will depend which traits come to the fore. If you are at work certain aspects of your personality may kick into gear and then when at home you let the guard down and another aspect of your personality is on show.

Another example could be, in a social context your outgoing Sanguine traits may shine and if you also have some melancholy traits, as part of your make up, you find yourself getting a little "peopled out" and look forward to going home to some peace and quiet. My wife has this balancing act as part of her personality make up.

We each have dominant personality traits and then secondary and third dimensions. In some people the traits of all four personalities are visible in differing measures.

These combinations of the personality traits are complimentary. They help to balance us out as individuals. Often people are attracted to people that are similar to themselves for socializing but when it comes to choosing partners, we are usually more attracted to the opposite personalities. For example you will often see an outgoing Choleric or Sanguine type partnered with a more introverted Melancholy or Phlegmatic person. In these relationships the differing personality traits compliment each other. Note that it is these differences that attracted us to each other that often cause us the most tension as well, as we see and do things differently.

As great dads, when you understand how your child is wired, you will know how best to relate to them. If you are a Sanguine personality and always spontaneous, fun-loving and cheeky, you may think twice about approaching your Melancholy son's Leggo collection that he has meticulously organized into same color and same size groupings, and play the throw them all in the air and see how they land game. You would exasperate your child because you have not respected how they are wired. You would do better to play with them within their mode of operating.

If you are a Phlegmatic dad wanting to simply chill quietly in the hammock and your Choleric daughter is busily trying to organize everyone, including you into a back yard game of soccer, you will either need to join in or clearly communicate to her why you are choosing not to play. She needs to know.

If your child is overtly Sanguine and all out for fun and social interaction, it is best not to assign them jobs to do where they will be working on their own for any length of time. They simply grow bored, and are quickly de-energized by being alone. You as the dad will only be frustrated, reading their behavior as lazy or selfish.

They, like everyone else, need to learn the value of work and contributing to the running of the household. You just need to package it in a Sanguine-engaging way. Depending on their age, dressing up into the appropriate work gear together is a good start, boots gloves, hat, overalls or whatever. Secondly the "let's do this together" approach will work far better because there is the social aspect to the task. The task will be all the more enticing to the Sanguine child, if you make it fun or offer the promise of fun together after you get the job done. For example you could say "I need your help to mow the lawn and then when the grass is cut we could make a slippery plastic slide with some soap suds and water for everyone to slide on." Be sure to follow through on any promises you ever make to any child.

The Choleric child will like to see achievement and progress. Creating a star chart will be a good motivator for them. When they do their chores or their homework, or do something special for someone else they get a star on their chart. Achieving their full quota of stars will be a reward in itself for the Choleric child. A small token gift or outing will be a bonus motivation for them.

The Sanguine child will be fully motivated by the gift or social outing, and as long as the stars are bright and the chart is colorful, it will engage them. The Melancholy child will want to place the stars on the chart themselves to ensure neatness, colour-coordination and consistency on the lines. Be sure to let them design and decorate the chart as part of the overall motivation. The Phlegmatic child will be enthusiastic at the start but will not be that excited after the first two or three stars are added.

Similarly when disciplining your child, consider their temperament. For a Sanguine child who thrives on social contact, 10-20 minutes in isolation may be a huge penalty. It may make them think twice about being naughty next time. However a Melancholy child may love the opportunity for that same length of time in peace and quiet. You would need to find a suitable alternative disciplinary measure for them. For a busy, on the go Choleric child who thrives on activity, having to sit still facing a corner for any length of time is an appropriate discipline. They will despise the waste of time, the sitting still and the not being able to do anything. They may reconsider their behaviour when they know the consequences.

To learn more about the personality types I recommend you read books like "Personality Plus" and "Different Children, Different Needs". Search for these on your computer. While searching, perhaps you could do some further reading by typing in the different personality types. It is beyond the scope of this book to explore every possible combination of the personality traits, every motivational technique or every disciplinary tactic.

For many people, making the discovery about personalities is very exciting. I have only offered a brief introduction here, in the context of understanding, and being able to better relate to our children. If this is of significant interest to you, further research could be very rewarding.

Each child is unique, but there are common behaviors among children with similar personalities. Learn to understand your child's personality and you will become far more effective in relating to them personally. You will gain greater insight into how to effectively discipline them according to their personality type. You will also be more effective in motivating them to clean up after themselves and generally help out around the home. That in itself has to be worth the investment.

When I coach individual parents, firstly we determine their own personality. We then look at each child in the family and gauge their personality. Together we determine strategies for building the relationship, employing effective discipline and finding ways to motivate the child to their success. Perhaps some parent coaching would be a worthwhile investment for you to consider in the pursuit of being a Great Dad. I would recommend you seek out a life coach that covers family relationships.

I find the personalities of people to be most fascinating and it makes for great conversation. Discover these together with each of your family members and work colleagues and watch the dynamics of your relationships improve dramatically. Discover the personalities of your children to unlock the greater potential of your relationship with them. They will value the fact that you understand them so much better and that you make a more concerted effort to relate to them as unique individuals.

CHAPTER 14

Final Thoughts

The greatest gift you can give your children is time. Material possessions are of some value. Gifts are nice. Acts of kindness are appreciated. But when you are a child, nothing beats having your dad wanting to regularly spend time with you just for the fun of it.

It has been a great pleasure to share with you some of my experiences in life as a dad. I hope that the many practical suggestions I have made will give you some fresh ideas for your fathering. It is my hope that your effectiveness as a father increases as you apply them in your relationship with your children.

Writing a book does require a big effort and the fact that you are reading this copy means that it actually got published which is a thrill to me.

While I have been passionate about effective fatherhood for many years, I have no doubt that the confronting ordeal of a life-threatening diagnosis and the subsequent journey has been the catalyst for me to write this book.

I encourage you as a dad to live your life on the front foot. Take every opportunity life has given you to be great, especially in the area of fatherhood.

Your kids are so incredibly important and they deserve you to be fully on your game. When it comes to your kids, being a good dad is one thing, being a great dad is everything!

Wherever possible, invest in your marriage, or if not married, then the relationship you share with your "significant other". This relationship is both of great worth to you, but it is also a living example to your children of how to build and maintain a healthy relationship. If you are a single dad there will be other aspects of relationship building that you will be displaying for your children.

The greatest gift you can give your children is time. Material possessions are of some value. Gifts are nice. Acts of kindness are appreciated. But when you are a child, nothing beats having your dad wanting to regularly spend time with you just for the fun of it.

Reach out to your own dad. He may have been an awesome dad. He may have been pretty average, or even below par. What is past is past. Today and tomorrow are all you can work with, so perhaps there is scope to build something a bit more meaningful with each other for the years ahead.

I was heartened recently when a 40 year-old father, together with his 67 year-old dad, attended one of my fatherhood seminars. They approached me afterwards and told me of their relationship, and how the grandchildren are benefitting from their ongoing mate-ship.

I love to hear from other men about their lives and about their relationships with their dads and with their children. I find most of them very inspiring and heart warming.

I would love to hear from you. I would like to hear what you have gained from reading this book and how it has added to your life and parenting.

Please inspire me, and the Good Dads GREAT DADS online community, by telling us what you're doing to be a great dad in the lives of your children or how this book has influenced you.

My contact details are www.gooddadsgreatdads.com

Life is relatively short and we each need to make the absolute most of every minute. Life is a precious gift and so are our children.

May you always be striving to be the greatest dad you can possibly be.

Your children are counting on you.

There are more publications from Good dads GREAT DADS coming your way.

If you would like to stay in touch simply like and share the Good Dads GREAT DADS Facebook page.

For regular encouragement on being a GREAT DAD be sure to Follow my blog at gooddadsgreatdads.com

Printed in Australia
AUOC02n1640041213
258929AU00003B/3/P